WORDS

A Dozen Biblical Words That Probably Don't Mean What You Think They Mean

by

Kenneth N. Myers

WORDS

© Copyright 2021 by Kenneth N. Myers

Myers, Kenneth Neal, 1959-
WORDS/Kenneth N. Myers

Cover design: Michael Peterson
Published by Mayeux Press
561 Bailey Drive, Denison TX 75021

Mayeux Press
DENISON, TEXAS

For Deacon Bill and Lois Jennings

Table of Content

Foreword

Foreword, not forward. The word before the words.

Words are important. Words mean things. Words have an almost magical ability to take a thought or idea in one person's mind and somehow through the power of speech and hearing implant that thought or idea into another person's mind.

Let me show you what I'm talking about. I'm going to think of an image in my mind, and then, almost by magic, I'm going to move that image from my mind into yours. And I won't even say abracadabra. OK. Ready?

Wait for it...

Do you know the image now? No, of course not, because I haven't done the magic yet. Ready?

Wait for it...

Orangutan.

Amazing, isn't it? You didn't know what image was in my mind, but through the power of a word I took that image out of my mind and transported it to yours. But, it gets better:

It is an old orangutan wearing a tie die t-shirt and eating cherry pie with a fork while sitting in a treehouse high in a jungle tree, a cup of coffee on the little wooden table by his side, which he picks up and sips from time to time while gazing down at the gazelles on the savannah far down below, as the sun slowly rises over the horizon.

Not only did I transport the idea of an orangutan from my brain to your brain, I transported an entire scene. THAT is the power of words.

We do it every day, we just don't think about the magic of it. In fact, the absolutely number one way we communicate with each other is through words.

But words are strange and somehow living creatures. They have ancestry, they have DNA, they are born, they grow, they change, they develop, and sometimes they die - no one uses the word bakemeats anymore, or wimples, although they were both common words in the 17th century and both made it into the King James Version of the Bible, along with bewray, broid, chambering, divers, graff, haply, trow, and a lot more. Those words are either dead or dying, and at the same time new words are being born and growing up, words like online, email, Covid, contactless, dox, and toyetic. Don't know what that last one means? Google it.

Ever since I was a little boy I have had a love affair with words. I remember as a pre-teen sitting in my room with a dictionary, reading it like a book (nerd confession). I am especially intrigued by the genealogy of words, where they came from, how they got here. Serendipity is one of my favorites. We all understand it to mean a kind of fortunate chance happening. But did you know that it comes from the word Serendip which was the old name for Sri Lanka? There is an old Arab fairy tale called *The Three Princes of Serendip*, and in the story the princes kept having wonderful, beneficial, seemingly coincidental things happen to them. The English lord Horace Walpole wrote a friend, referenced the story, and said he had experienced an event of "serendipity." That was 1754. The word stuck, and is still being used today. Fortuitous, no?

Some words also change, and some change so completely that today they mean exactly the opposite of their original meaning. Let is a great example. When it was used in the King James Version of the Bible (1611) it meant to forbid. Now it means to allow. Leech used to mean a doctor or miracle worker. Now it means a slimy creature that medieval doctors used to suck blood out of patients. Silly used to mean pious. Now it just means silly.

Words are also the primary way God reveals himself and communicates to us humans. In fact (more about this later), the Gospel of John tells us, "In the beginning was the Word, and the Word was with God, and the Word was God." (John 1.1)

As it happens, we now have an entire book, well, a collection of books, called the Bible (*biblia* in Greek, meaning, well, a collection of books) that is completely filled with words that communicate to us something about God and his people.

On one level, almost anyone can pick up a Bible, read it, and discover truth. But there is a deeper level of understanding awaiting those willing to do the hard work of digging down into the depths of what a word means, if you will, below the surface. This is particularly true when it comes to translations. John 1.1 in English tells us, "In the beginning was the Word…" The Greek word for word is *logos*. And it is packed full of meaning that impacts our understanding of what John was getting at, which will be completely lost on the person who doesn't do the hard work of research.

In this book, I have done the hard work for you. And I have put it all together into an easy, insightful, and hopefully enjoyable read. I present here a dozen or so biblical words that on the surface mean one thing, but digging deeper shows a much more profound meaning, and sometimes even a meaning completely at odds with how we understand the English word today (propitiation is a good example).

Much of the material in this book is found in other books I have written, and I almost decided to not write this book because the information was already addressed elsewhere. But friends of mine encouraged me to collect these words into a single volume that could be easily accessed without having to scrounge through my other writings to find them.

And so, I present to you this little volume which can be read straight through, or in bits and pieces. You can begin at the beginning or jump to a chapter that intrigues you. I pray that you are blessed and enriched as you read, and that you fall more in love with God, and the words he uses to communicate truth to us.

Merida, Yucatan, November 2021

Chapter One
Word

(Adapted from *The Trinity Untangled*, Chapter Four)

Most of the time when modern Christians say, "The Word of God," they are referring to the Bible. That's all well and good, but when the Bible itself (both Old and New Testaments) refer to the Word of God it isn't making a self-referential statement. For example, when we read in Hebrews 4.12 that, "the word of God is living and active, sharper than any two-edged sword, piercing to the division of soul and of spirit, of joints and of marrow, and discerning the thoughts and intentions of the heart," we are making a significant mistake if we think the writer is referring to Scripture. The phrase meant something different to the Apostles and those who came before them, and its roots go all the way back to the first chapter of Genesis.

OK. Time for a joke. An old drunk was walking home from the bar late one night and decided to take a shortcut through the cemetery. In his condition and in the dark, he fell into an open, freshly dug grave. He spent about an hour trying to climb out but kept falling back to the floor of the grave and he finally resigned himself to curl up in the corner, spend the night there, and wait for help in the morning. A little later another drunk made the same mistake. For about ten minutes he feverishly tried to climb his way out. From the pitch black corner the first drunk said, "You'll never get out of here." But he did.

Our speaking is a revelation of our presence.

The Word in Creation

The very first self-revelation of the unknowable/unseeable/untouchable God was when he spoke. The first time we *see* God, the first time he makes himself known, is when he *says* something, and that something was, "Let there be light." Ten times in the first chapter of the Bible we read, "And God said..." God's *Word* and God's *Being* cannot be separated. Karl Barth wrote, "God's word is God himself in revelation."[1]

According to Scripture, God's Word *is* the power that brought about the universe. Genesis records that "God said..," but the Psalmist penned, "By *the word of the Lord* the heavens were made, And by the breath

---

[1] Barth, Karl, *Church Dogmatics*, Volume 1; Edinburg, T & T Clark, 1960; p. 339.

of His mouth all their host" (33.6). "The word of Yahweh is a creative agent, and it is fulfilled in the visible creation that results from it."[2]

It is important to see that behind the divine speaking is divine power and authority. The Word of God comes forth from the inner depths of the unknowable/unseeable/untouchable God - from the Father - and carries with it the power of God to accomplish God's will and purpose. So, through the prophet Isaiah God can say, "so shall *my word* be that goes out from my mouth; it shall not return to me empty, but it shall accomplish that which I purpose, and shall succeed in the thing for which I sent it" (Isaiah 55.11)

So, creation itself is the result of the transcendent God manifesting himself through his Word, and in making himself known he creates out of nothing (except the

2 Fortman, Edmund J., *The Triune God*, Grand Rapids, Baker, 1972, p. 4.

power of his Word) this magnificent "other than him" that we call the universe and everything in it.

The Prophets

92 times in the Old Testament we find the phrase, "the Word of the Lord came to…" The first use of the phrase is in Genesis 15.1: "After these things *the word of the Lord* came to Abram in a vision, saying,'Do not fear, Abram, I am a shield to you; Your reward shall be very great.'" God, the Word of God, came to Abraham. God spoke, and revealed himself. God's Word is God himself in revelation. Let's take a quick romp through the Old Testament and see how the phrase is used.

It is used twice in Genesis (15.1,4), then the rest of the Pentateuch (the first five books of the Bible, the "Books of Moses") does not use the phrase in this way. But when we reach the historical books, when the office of the prophet reaches its ascendancy, it appears again in a stronger way. I am going to list eight examples. The tendency people have when they come to a list of Scriptures in a theology book is to just skim over them and not really pay attention. I am begging you to read them and think about them. See what they are saying.

- 1 Samuel 3.2: And the Lord appeared again at Shiloh, for the Lord revealed himself to Samuel at Shiloh by *the word of the Lord*.

- 1 Samuel 15.10: *The word of the Lord* came to Samuel...

- 2 Samuel 7.4: But that same night *the word of the Lord* came to Nathan...

- 2 Samuel 24.11: And when David arose in the morning, *the word of the Lord* came to the prophet Gad, David's seer...

- 1 Kings 6.11: Now *the word of the Lord* came to Solomon…

- 1 Kings 13.20: And as they sat at the table, *the word of the Lord* came to the prophet who had brought him back.
- 1 Kings 16.1: And *the word of the Lord* came to Jehu the son of Hanani against Baasha.

- 1 Kings 18.1: After many days the word of the Lord came to Elijah, in the third year, saying, "Go, show yourself to Ahab, and I will send rain upon the earth."

- 1 Chronicles 17.3: But that same night *the word of the Lord* came to Nathan…

In every instance, God *himself* comes to someone through the Word of the Lord. God reveals himself through his Word. His Word *is* his revelation, *is* him.

The Wisdom books use the phrase sparingly (we have already seen Psalm 33.6: "By *the word of the Lord* the heavens were made, and by the breath of his mouth all their host."), then the phrase goes full steam in the writings of the prophets, where it became the imprimatur of God stamped onto the ministry or the prophetic utterance of the various prophets. Notice, in the following list, how many of the prophetic books actually begin with the phrase.

- Isaiah 38.4: Then *the word of the Lord* came to Isaiah…

- Jeremiah 1.11: And *the word of the Lord* came to me, saying, "Jeremiah, what do you see?" And I said, "I see an almond branch."

- Ezekiel 1.3: *the word of the Lord* came to Ezekiel the priest, the son of Buzi, in the land of the Chaldeans by the Chebar canal, and the hand of the Lord was upon him there.

- Ezekiel makes use of it more than anyone - fifty times he says, "The *word of the Lord* came to me."

- Joel 1.1: *The word of the Lord* that came to Joel, the son of Pethuel...

- Jonah 1.1: Now *the word of the Lord* came to Jonah the son of Amittai...

- Micah 1.1: *The word of the Lord* that came to Micah of Moresheth...

- Zephaniah 1.1: *The word of the Lord* that came to Zephaniah the son of Cushi...

- Zechariah 1.1: In the eighth month, in the second year of Darius, *the word of the Lord* came to the prophet Zechariah...

- Malachi 1.1: The oracle of *the word of the Lord* to Israel by Malachi...

It becomes clear that the primary phrase of revelation in the Old Testament is, "the Word of the Lord came to..." When the Word of the Lord comes to someone, it is God himself coming to someone. God's Word is his revelation. The Word of the Lord *is* the Lord!

The Logos

When the Jewish world started interacting with the Greek world, and when more Jews spoke Greek than spoke Hebrew or Aramaic, the Scriptures were for the first time translated into the Greek language. Called the *Septuagint* (*LXX* for an abbreviation), it was translated by Jewish scholars in Alexandria, Egypt, and by the time of Christ and the Apostles had become the commonly used version (every Old Testament quote found in the New

Testament is from the *LXX*). The *LXX* uses the Greek word *logos* for "word," and it also carries with it a long and complex history from the world of Greek philosophy. *Logos* means "word," "not in the grammatical sense, but...a word which, uttered by a living voice, embodies a conception of idea."[3]

At the time when Jesus was a boy growing up in Egypt, there lived a brilliant Jewish philosopher named Philo who attempted to unite the Jewish religion and Greek philosophy (one has to at least wonder if the little boy Jesus ever met the wise old philosopher). He found that this idea of "the Word" was common to both traditions, and spent a lot of his time building a case that the Greeks and Jews were pointing to the same thing. Philo saw the *logos* as a kind of mediating figure which comes from God, and which brings the transcendent (unknowable/unseeable/

---

[3] Thayer, Joseph Henry, *Greek-English Lexicon of the New Testament*, Grand Rapids, Zondervan, 1974, p. 358.

untouchable) God close to his creation. In other words, in the *logos*, God becomes immanent. In an odd twist (remember, this is *before* the New Testament was written), Philo also sees the *logos* as one who represents all of humanity as a high priest and advocate before the transcendent God. The *logos*, for Philo (and because of him, for much of the Jewish thinking world), "is the sum and locus of God's creative power, and as such it orders and governs the visible world."[4]

So through Philo, at precisely the time that Christ was born, the Jewish scholars were seeing the Word of the Lord through slightly adjusted lenses, and recognizing that this Word who kept showing up in the Old Testament writings was a mediating, immanent presence of God himself.

---

[4] Kittel, v 4, p. 89.

The Gospel of John

There are four Gospels in the Bible. The first three are very similar, and called the Synoptic ("with the same eye") Gospels. The fourth, the Gospel of John, is different from the rest and has a decidedly more philosophical and theological feel to it. Whereas the other Gospels begin with the birth of Jesus, John lays hold of Philo's ideas, of Greek thought, of Jewish theology, and begins his Gospel with the famous phrase, "In the beginning was the Word (*logos*), and the Word was with God, and the Word was God."

Every well schooled Greek or Jew who read these words would instantly identify them with the *logos* of Greek philosophy and of Philo, and would immediately associate these words with the Old Testament "the Word of the Lord" who brought the world into existence and spoke to the Prophets. So far, so good. John isn't saying anything in this verse that is different than Philo. The Word was in the beginning. The Word was alongside God (shall we say coming forth from God). The Word *was* God! But then, in verse 14, John blows the lid off the philosophical / theological can: "And the Word *became flesh* and dwelt among us, and we have seen his glory, glory as of the only Son from the Father, full of grace and truth." God became human! The baby who's birth story is so beautifully told in the Gospel of Luke is the Word of God himself. God the Son, who reveals the glory of God to us. In his delightful book, *God Came Near*, Max Lucado offers 25 questions he would like to ask the Virgin Mary. The best one is the last one: "Did you ever think, That's God eating my soup?"

After the first chapter of John, the New Testament never again refers to Jesus as the Word until the end of Revelation, where we read, "And He is clothed with a robe dipped in blood; and His name is called The Word of God" (19.13).

The early leaders of the Church laid hold of this concept of the Word of God, the *logos*, and made much use of it. Justin Martyr (a Syrian Christian who was martyred in 165) wrote, "Since God is transcendent, the *logos* bridges the abyss between God and man."[5] St. Basil the Great (the bishop of Caesarea who died in 379) tells us that the Son is called the Word, "so that it be clear that he proceeded from the mind [of God]…because he is the image of his generator, *showing in himself the entire generator.*"[6] Gregory of Nazianzus (who's thinking was so formative for the development of Trinitarian doctrine) wrote that the Son is called the Word, "because he is related to the Father as word to mind… because of the union, and of his declaratory function…the Son is a concise demonstration and easy setting forth of the Father's nature."[7]

---

[5] Justin Martyr, *Apologia*, 32.8

[6] Basil of Caesarea, *Homilies*, 16.3.

[7] Gregory of Nazianzus, *Orations*, 30.20.

Paul Tillich wrote, "*Logos* is the principle of the self-manifestation of God...
Therefore, whenever God appears, either to himself or to others outside himself, it is the *Logos* which appears."[8]

The Word is the bringing forth of the mind. We think something, but until we articulate it, it remains invisible and unknowable, internalized. The Word of the Lord, that is, God the Son, is the bringing forth of the "inner God," that is, God the Father. The Word is the revelation of God himself. God, making himself known. God the Father reveals himself *only* through God the Son.

---

[8] Tillich, Paul, *A History of Christian Thought*, New York, Simon and Schuster, p. 30.

Chapter Two
Remembrance
(Adapted from *How Christians Worship*, Chapter Fourteen)

When we rounded the magical corner first discovered that late summer night many years before, the Art Cafe had changed. Julian was still there, but no food was to be had. He had closed the cafe to focus on an art project which might well be his life's greatest achievement: a fifty portfolio tribute for the 400th anniversary of Cervantes' *Don Quixote*, composed of handmade paper, calligraphy, pen and ink drawings, and watercolors - all envisioned by Julian, but brought to life by a team of more than a dozen skilled craftsmen and artists. Disappointed that there would be no dinner but intrigued by the project, Victor,

Eight years before, on a summer evening in the year 2000, my son Ken and I were lost in a foreign city, hadn't had dinner, and were famished. The streets on a map of Toledo, Spain look a lot like a bowl of spaghetti, not a straight lane in the whole place and roads crossing over themselves at least a half dozen times. We had explored the ancient town for an entire day, making our way on foot from one magnificent piece of history to the next, but we had no idea where we were when, in search of late night nourishment, we rounded the corner and found with a stroke of serendipity the Art Cafe. Half art gallery, half bistro, we walked into the little four table establishment and had the place to ourselves. Rather than ordering from the menu, we asked the owner/chef - Julian Simon - to bring us what he thought best, and his eyes twinkled at the opportunity. First, he chose a bottle of wine - a vintage from Ribera del Duero, he told us, a region at the time undiscovered by the rest of the world but loved by Spanish wine connoisseurs. Half an hour later he rounded the corner carrying a tray laden with the best of fare - gazpacho according to his mother's recipe, Spanish sausage made in the old style, dishes of vegetables and beef spiced and cooked to perfection - and he stood there with a look of anticipation as we had our first tastes. Heaven exploded on our tongues. "I use only the best ingredients," he said, "and I prepare it in the old tradition." It was the best meal I have ever eaten.

A year later, when I returned with my wife, I was concerned that I had built up the moment in my mind and perhaps overstated the case for Julian and his culinary skills. I was wrong. It was the second best meal I have ever eaten. Later, my son Ken and his wife Megan went back to Toledo for their honeymoon. I called over and arranged dinner with Julian, and he treated them like royalty on their special occasion.

Back in Spain for the first time in seven years, Shirley and I insisted on taking our close friends, restauranteurs Victor and Debbie Leal, to my favorite restaurant on the planet. But when we walked into the Art Cafe Julian informed us that it was no longer a restaurant, and was instead a simple wine bar. With all his energy being spent on the art project, he had no time to maintain the food service. But that same day, enchantment struck again.

Julian said that although he could not offer us food, he did have wine. His wife sat down at the table and Julian disappeared to a back room. When he returned, there was that familiar twinkle in his eyes which had endeared me to him when we first met. He held in his hand a bottle of wine and looked at me as if I should notice something. "What?" I asked, and he said, "This is the same wine I served you when you first came eight years ago. It is the last bottle, and I have been saving it for a special occasion!" We sat for hours, Julian passionately explaining his art project, Victor and him talking about the culinary crafts, everyone enjoying old and new friends. When the time came to leave, I asked what the cost was for the wine. Julian cast a frown my way, as if I had insulted him, and said, "If you drink alone, you pay me. If I drink with you, you are in my home, you are my guests!"

Saying goodbye and walking out the door, I turned and asked, "Julian, I've told my friends all about your food - where else in Toledo can I find that quality of gazpacho?"

"It is impossible!," he exclaimed with his strong Spanish accent. "But you return in three hours and we have gazpacho!"

"No! I didn't mean for you to make gazpacho for us! I was just asking for recommendations of another place."

"OK," he said, "you come back, or you don't come back. Either way, I will have gazpacho!"

Three hours later we returned to a mini-feast of the best gazpacho in the world, and another hour or two of wonderful conversation.

Julian is one of the most passionate people I know; he puts himself wholeheartedly into everything he does, whether it is cooking or entertaining or crafting a great piece of art. When it comes to food, Julian understands that presentation is every bit as important as taste. What separates dinner at the Art Cafe from a great meal in some other restaurant is one simple truth that Julian knows by heart: Dining is theater.

The difference between a good meal and a great meal is not just about the quality of food; a great meal is theatrical. There is art involved; presentation is important; it isn't just a nourishment for the body, it is a feast for the taste buds and for the eyes; conversation is had, lines are delivered, and *fellowship* happens.

In Christian worship, the most important act in the play is Act Three, The Service Of The Table. Like the movie *Babette's Feast*, the whole drama builds to the dinner. We come as the people of God to give thanks (*Eucharist* is simply the Greek word for *thanksgiving*) to God for all his benefits toward us, chiefly for what he did for us in offering his Son Jesus Christ for the reconciliation of the world to himself, and we share at table with one another and with God.

A Short History of Holy Communion

It could be said (and the early Fathers *did* say) that the Eucharist has its roots in the Tree of Life in the Garden of Eden. But as a table-meal, the Eucharist finds its beginning in the friendship meal of Jewish rabbis and their students. A teacher and his disciples would gather together, follow a traditional ceremony during a meal, and discuss things of spiritual importance. There is some evidence that the standard number for these groups was the teacher and a dozen disciples, honoring Israel and his twelve sons.

Our celebration of Holy Communion has even deeper roots in the Jewish Passover, a ceremonial meal commanded by God as the children of Israel were preparing to be delivered out of slavery in Egypt and brought into freedom in the Promise Land. God ordered Moses to have the people prepare a lamb, eat it standing, and be ready to hurriedly escape the bondage of Pharaoh. They were to eat the flesh of the lamb, and mark their doors with its blood, that the Angel of Lord might *pass over* them and their lives be saved (Exodus 12). Every year this meal was celebrated as an enduring feast, and became the central act of Jewish worship.

When Jesus gathered his twelve disciples for his final meal with them, it was a combination of these two things - the celebration of the Passover meal, and the celebration of the friendship meal. The four Gospels don't all record all the stories about Jesus. Mark and John have nothing about his birth, for example, but all four Gospels recount the story of Jesus establishing the sacrament of Holy Communion (Matthew 26, Mark 4, Luke 22, John 13). Saint Paul also records the story of Christ instituting the Eucharist (1 Corinthians 11.22-26) and shows that already, early in the life of the Church, the celebration of the Lord's Table was central to the Church's worship of God.

Two things should be noticed in Paul's version of the story. First, he says that he "received from the Lord" the tradition of Holy Communion. Somehow, in some context, the resurrected and ascended Christ instructed Paul about this meal (remember, Paul was a persecutor of the Church and converted several years after the resurrection; Acts 9). However this encounter happened, when Paul wrote about it, he used the same words as the Gospels:

> The Lord Jesus, on the night he was betrayed, took bread, and when he had given thanks, he broke it and said, "This is my body, which is for you; do this in remembrance of me." In the same way, after supper he took the cup, saying, "This cup is the new covenant in my blood; do this, whenever you drink it, in

remembrance of me." (1 Corinthians 11.22-25)

Then Paul adds, "For whenever you eat this bread and drink this cup, you proclaim the Lord's death until he comes" (v. 26). Far from being a meal to be casually observed whenever the pastor thinks it important enough to get around to, this meal was specifically given by Jesus not only to the original disciples, but also to the late-comer Paul, who would bring the Gospel to the Gentiles.

Second, notice the language Paul uses: "for I *received* (*parelabon*) from the Lord what I also *passed on* (*paredoka*)to you" (v. 23). This is not Paul saying, "hey, let me tell you what Jesus told me". He uses two specific technical words for *the transmission of tradition*. Some modern Christians may shy away from observing traditions, opting instead for a looser structure of sudden inspiration, but in this they part ways with Paul and the other Apostles.

Throughout the entire New Testament era, the history of the early Church, and the first sixteen centuries of Christian faith, the celebration of the Holy Eucharist has been *the central act* of Christian worship. Though abused in the medieval era and ignored (or at least sidelined) by much of the modern Protestant church, in our time Christians from all traditions are rediscovering the importance and centrality of the Lord's Supper and returning to its celebration as the core of worship.

What Happens In Communion?

The Thirty Nine Articles state,

> The Supper of the Lord is not only a sign of the love that Christians ought to have among themselves one to another, but rather it is a Sacrament of our Redemption by Christ's death: insomuch that to such as rightly,

worthily, and with faith, receive the same, the Bread which we break is a partaking of the Body of Christ; and likewise the Cup of Blessing is a partaking of the Blood of Christ. (Article 28)

The Church, particularly in the West, has gotten bogged down with philosophical technicalities in attempting to explain the *mystery* of what happens at the altar (can a mystery really be explained?). At one end of the debate, Roman Catholics believe in the dogma of *transubstantiation* - that the physical bread and wine change substance and become the physical body and blood of Christ. On the other end of the debate, some Protestants (following Zwingli) insist that *nothing* happens, and we are eating and drinking only bread and wine as a kind of physical symbol devoid of sacramental reality. The bread is nothing but bread. The wine is nothing but wine - or better, grape juice - a novelty introduced into the Church by Methodist minister,

Thomas Bramwell Welch, his pasteurized juice first marketed as *Dr. Welch's Unfermented Wine* in 1869. It is all mere symbol (which brings to mind the famous line by the female American novelist Flannery O'Connor, who, arguing that if communion were only a picture of Christ's passion, it was a very unconvincing portrayal, said, "If it is only a symbol, then to hell with it.").

The early Church, (and later the Orthodox in the East and the Anglicans in the west) made no attempt to explain *how* the mystery happened, only insisting *that* the mystery happened. The bread becomes the Body of Christ. The wine becomes the Blood of Jesus. Christ is *really* in the sacrament. Thus, the term, *Real Presence*.

Two words in the New Testament are important contributions in embracing the mystery. The first is *participate*. Saint Paul wrote,

I speak to sensible people; judge for yourselves what I say. Is not the cup of thanksgiving for which we give thanks a *participation* in the blood of Christ? And is not the bread that we break a *participation* in the body of Christ? (1 Corinthians 10.15f)

Participation here is *koinonia*, meaning "fellowship" or "to have communion with" (hence the term *Communion*). It carries the idea of partnership, having a share in a thing. If you own a building with a group of partners, it doesn't mean that you own the bathroom and someone else owns the hallway and someone else owns the office and someone else owns the storeroom. It means that you all own the whole building together. If you have stock in the Welch's Grape Juice company, it doesn't mean that you own the bottling machinery and someone else owns the pasteurizing vats and someone else owns the labels. You all own the whole company together.

When we are in Christ we are partners with him; we have *koinonia* with him and with one another. When the faithful approach the Table of the Lord they *share* in - own shares in - his sacrifice to the Father, and enjoy the benefits procured by him. Paul insists that the bread and the wine is a true fellowship with the Body and Blood of Christ. When we receive communion, what is ours is his (our weaknesses, sinfulness, frailty, humanity; our victories, loves, devotion), and what is his is ours (his suffering, crucifixion, death; his resurrection, exaltation, enthronement in heaven, victory over sin and defeat of Satan and death - and yes, his life giving Spirit). *This* is what happens in the Great Thanksgiving we offer to God!

The second important biblical word is *remembrance* or *remember*. Thousands of churches around the world, which embrace the Zwinglian notion of the *real absence* of Christ in the bread and the wine, nevertheless have carved into their

Communion tables, "Do this in remembrance of me" (quoting 1 Corinthians 11.24). If they knew what it meant, they might sandblast the words away.

The Greek word is *anamnesis*, and it doesn't mean what most people think it means. It doesn't mean to fondly remember a thing or to mentally recollect a past event. In fact, actualizing that definition is an impossibility for us. If I were to ask you, "Do you remember when Christopher Columbus planted the Spanish flag on a beach in the Bahamas and claimed it for Ferdinand and Isabela?" your answer would certainly be, "No." You may *know* *about* it, but you don't *remember* it because it happened on October 12, 1492, and you weren't there! Neither do you remember Jesus dying on the cross. You weren't there. You may know about it, meditate on in, believe it, and understand it, but you don't remember it.

But *anamnesis* doesn't mean to recollect an event. It means to "make present the past which can never remain merely past but becomes effective in the present."[9]

The word comes over into English in the medical field: *anamnestic reaction*: "a renewed rapid production of an antibody on the second (or subsequent) encounter with the same antigen." I bet that is as clear as mud! So, unless you are nurse or a doctor, let me put it in plain English. An anamnestic reaction goes something like this: you are out enjoying a picnic with your sweetheart and a nasty old red wasp stings the living daylights out of you. Bang! Ouch! Right on the ear. What you didn't know, because you've never been stung by a nasty old red wasp, is that you are deathly allergic to it. You swell up, turn red, your heart beats faster and you have to go to the emergency room for a shot lest

---

[9] Balz & Schneider, *Exegetical Dictionary of the New Testament*, Grand Rapids, Eerdmans, 1990; Volume I, p. 85.

you go into anaphylactic shock. Five years later, you are out boating, enjoying a nice summer day with your sweetheart, and another nasty old red wasp sneaks up and hits you on your thigh. Only this time, something really strange happens: your ear swells up like it has just been stung too. It hasn't of course; it was stung five years ago, but that sting from the past "happens again" and now it is like you have been stung twice. *This*, my friends, is an *anamnestic reaction*.

And *this* is the word Jesus used when he said, "Do this in remembrance - in *anamnesis* - of me."

Every time we come to the Table, we experience a re-presentation of Christ and his sacrifice; we are entering into that once and for all singular offering of Christ to God which happened 2000 years ago on a hill outside Jerusalem, but which transcends time and space and is therefore eternal - we enter into the eternal moment of that singular sacrifice. Each time we celebrate the Eucharist we offer thanks to God for the reconciling death and resurrection of Jesus, and *his death and resurrection become effective for us in the here and now*. The benefit is not contingent on our understanding it or on our emotional condition; it just *is*. We don't try to close our eyes and furrow our brows and *remember* something we weren't there for, we just experience his presence - his Body, his Blood, his sacrifice, his victory - in the act of Holy Communion.

The next time you receive Holy Communion, you don't have to *try* to *remember*. You are simply participating in all that Christ is and all that he has done, and you are bringing it into the reality of now.

Chapter Three
Daily

(Adapted from *How Christians Pray*, Chapter Five)

"Give us this day our daily bread…" The phrase is prayed by untold millions of Christians every day. It is the fourth petition in the Lord's Prayer, and the first one that turns the focus of prayer to our own needs. At first glance, you might think that "give us this day our daily bread" is the easiest petition to understand. It is just a prayer for God to feed us. But this is just the first glance, and a closer look will reveal that it may well be the most profound and complex of all the petitions. So, I'm warning you now, for the next few pages you are going to have to put on your theologian's hat and do some serious thinking. Ready? OK. Buckle up and hang on for the ride. Here we go.

What In The World does *Daily* Mean?

The big problem with this petition is that no one is sure what it means. Seriously! And here is where the difficulty lies - the word *daily*. "It can't be that tough," you might say, "it means just what it says - daily. It means today, tomorrow, the next day, every day. Lord, give us what we need each and every day." Oh, sure, you know what the word means in your *own* language, but let's talk for a minute about the language the Bible was written in, Greek.

You see, the Greek word for daily is *epiousios*, and it isn't used *anywhere* else in the whole Bible, or *anywhere* else in Greek literature and writing. It isn't used *anywhere else at all*! The *only* place it is ever used - ever - is in the Lord's Prayer! How do you define a word that isn't used elsewhere? There is nothing to compare it to; there are no parallel uses in other writings. It seems that Jesus, or the Gospel writers, made it up on the spot!

The word *epiousios* is a compound word combining the prefix *epi*, which means "over" or "above" or "super" (think of *epidermis* - the skin over the rest of your skin, or *epicenter* - the place that is directly above the center of an earthquake), with the root word *ousios*, which means "substance" or "essence" or "being". Put it all together and it becomes as clear as mud: do we translate it "super-substantial" or "more than essential", or some other combination of words? Church fathers, Bible scholars, linguists and regular folk have been tackling the word for centuries. And they've boiled it down to three possibilities.

The first possibility is that the phrase means "give us today the bread which is essential for today". The second possibility is that it means "we're praying today that you will give us tomorrow's bread", and the third possibility is that it means, "give us today the supernatural bread - the heavenly bread - the transcendent bread". You can pick whichever you like (and whichever you choose, you will find yourself in good company). As for me, I'm going to choose all three (and I will keep company with Saint Augustine on this one)! I believe the Holy Spirit inspired the Scriptures, and he inspired the writers of the Gospels to use this word and not another. In other words, the Holy Spirit inspired the ambiguity! So, let's take it as a possibility that God wants us to understand this one word to mean all three things.

Bread for Today

With this petition we start speaking to God about things in our own lives. The Bible tells us to "Delight yourself in the Lord and he will give you the desires of your heart" (Psalm 37.4). If we delight ourselves in the Lord (in other words, if we have truly prayed from our hearts that God's name be hallowed, his kingdom come, his will be done) then our desires will not be out of keeping with his will. Our desires will line up with his desires and we can ask him and he will give us the desires of our hearts. Obviously, survival is one of the desires of our hearts. When we pray for our daily bread, we are praying for everything we need for physical survival. "The bread signifies here not only bread as such, and not even food in general, but absolutely everything necessary for life, everything which makes possible our existence".[10]

---

[10] Schmemann, Alexander, p. 56

Some other religions (including some ancient Greek, some modern Buddhist, and some crazy pseudo-Christian) teach that God doesn't care about the physical creation (including our bodies), or that the physical world is a kind of trap that we should get free from by mortifying the body and ultimately dying and escaping the body. Christians, on the other hand, believe that God *made* the physical world (including our bodies), and that he called it "good" and "very good" (Genesis 1.31). Our bodies are every bit as important as our souls! Salvation is not achieved merely by our souls going to heaven, but it also includes our bodies being raised in immortality. So, it is very important to understand, praying for our bodies and the physical needs we have is just as spiritual as praying for our souls and the spiritual needs we have.

When we pray for God to give us our daily bread, we are clearly recognizing our dependence on God. I used to pastor a church in the dairy land of Wisconsin, and one of the men in the church hosted a "Farm Day" for inner city children who had never seen the countryside. Would you believe there were kids who didn't know that milk came from cows? They thought it came from the store!

Listen, milk comes from the store, but first it comes from cows, and in an even deeper sense it comes from God, who made the cows and the grass to feed them and the farmers to milk them! Our daily bread may come from a restaurant or a cozy kitchen, but before that it came from crushed grain grown in a field, and before that it came from God who gave the rain to make the grain grow and who created the farmer to harvest the grain. When we pray for God to give us our daily bread we are praying for the whole cycle of production - we are praying for peace and good weather and healthy farmers and a decent economy and all the other things necessary to put bread on our tables (or clothes on our backs, or water in our faucets - you get the picture). But more than all that, we are saying, "God, everything I need to exist ultimately comes from *you!*" This little petition is a petition of trust. We are declaring that we trust God to take care of us.

Just as soon as Jesus teaches the disciples how to pray this prayer, he adds,

> "And why do you worry about clothes? See how the lilies of the field grow. They do not labor or spin. Yet I tell you that not even Solomon in all his splendor was dressed like one of these. If that is how God clothes the grass of the field, which is here today and tomorrow is thrown into the fire, will he not much more clothe you, O you of little faith? So do not worry, saying, 'What shall we eat?' or 'What shall we drink?' or 'What shall we wear?' For the pagans run

after all these things, and your heavenly Father knows that you need them. But seek first his kingdom and his righteousness, and *all these things will be given to you as well."* (Matthew 6.28-33)

This petition teaches us two more things. It teaches us to pray for particulars and to pray for other's needs as well.

We pray for "bread" - what is the bread you need? For some it may be financial, for others it may be clothing, for others it will have to do with housing - whatever it is that we need, we ought to ask God for it, realizing that he is the true source of all our blessings.

And it is not just "my daily bread", it is "our daily bread" - so our prayers include all God's people. We pray for the needs of our families, our churches, our cities and nations, the poor. We pray for the whole world.

Tomorrow's Bread

The second way of translating the text is "give us this day our bread for tomorrow". On the one hand, we are praying for the necessities of life not just in this instant, but for tomorrow too. In the Jewish rhythm of time, the day began at sundown and continued until the next sundown. So, for example, a Jewish Sabbath would begin on what we call Friday night and would end at sundown Saturday. As an evening prayer, the Lord's Prayer says, "Lord, we've been blessed by you today, now a new day is beginning and we are putting our hope in you for that day as well." It isn't wrong to ask God for future blessings; it is wrong to fret and worry about this things. This prayer is saying "I trusted in you today, and I'm trusting in you tomorrow".

But of course "tomorrow" in the big picture - the *big tomorrow* - is the fullness of the Kingdom of Heaven. In other words, we are praying, "Lord, give us, in the here and now, the blessings that are laid up for us in heaven. Give us the favor of the coming Kingdom. Give us the inheritance won through Christ." Interestingly, the writer of Hebrews uses "bread language" when he describes our spiritual life: we are a people "who have *tasted* the heavenly gift, who have shared in the Holy Spirit, who have *tasted* the goodness of the word of God and the powers of *the coming age*." (Hebrews 6.4-5) We have only tasted what is to come, but the taste is so good that we cry out, "Give us more, Lord, give us more...give us this day the bread of Tomorrow!" The Psalmist knew of that rich flavor that is found only in trusting the Lord: "Taste and see that the Lord is good; blessed is the man who takes refuge in him." (Psalm 34.8)

Heavenly Bread

Finally, when we pray "give us this day our daily bread" we are asking God to give us that bread that is "supersubstantial".

Before going further, think for a moment about the central role that food plays in the Bible. In Genesis God gives Adam and Eve every fruit bearing tree (except for one) to supply them with food. The original sin involved eating. From that time forward food held a symbolic and spiritual meaning. Abraham tithes to the great priest Melchizedek who in turn gives him bread and wine. Esau sells his birthright for a bowl of soup. The enslaved Israelites ate a Passover meal before their deliverance from Egypt. David, in the most loved Psalm of all, says, "You prepare a table before me in the presence of my enemies." (Psalm 23.5) The sacrifices in the Temple are made up of what we eat: grain and lamb and beef.

All these things are interrelated, and in some fashion they point forward to *"The Feast"* - that great day of the restoration of all things. The prophet Isaiah foresaw it and wrote, "On this mountain the Lord Almighty will prepare a feast of rich food for all peoples, a banquet of aged wine - the best of meats and the finest of wines. On this mountain he will destroy the shroud that enfolds all peoples, the sheet that covers all nations; he will swallow up death forever. The Sovereign Lord will wipe away the tears from all faces; he will remove the disgrace of his people from all the earth. The Lord has spoken." (Isaiah 25.6-8) Jesus told many parables centered around the same theme: "The kingdom of heaven is like a king who prepared a wedding banquet for his son" (Matthew 22.2), he said. The Apostle John calls it "the wedding supper of the Lamb." (Revelation 19.9)

Do you see it? All this language is about salvation and restoration and being in the presence of God - all this language is about the *Kingdom of God* - and yet all this language is also about food. Now, watch this. In John chapter six we find the discourse of Jesus regarding the Bread of Life. It would do you well to put this book down and read that whole chapter. I'll wait here for you...

Jesus told his listeners, "I am the bread of life. Your forefathers ate the manna in the desert, yet they died. But here is the bread that comes down from heaven, which a man may eat and not die. I am the living bread that came down from heaven. If anyone eats of this bread, he will live forever." (John 6.48-51)

God had provided for their forefathers some mysterious bread while they wandered in the wilderness - they didn't know what it was, so they called it "manna" (which means, "what is it?"), and it was "bread from heaven" - which, interestingly, they gathered fresh every day (daily bread) - but it didn't keep them alive forever. They all died eventually. The true bread from heaven, Jesus told them, is himself. In other words, Jesus himself is the nourishment people need to sustain life. A relationship with God in the person of Jesus Christ is our hope, our salvation - our very *life*.

When we pray "give us this day our super-substantial bread", one of the things we are praying is, "Lord, give us *you*! Give us more of you. Deepen our walk with you. Increase our understanding of your ways. Lord, without you coming into our lives every day we don't even *have* lives."

That's easy enough to understand. Jesus is the bread of life, he is our spiritual nourishment. But then Jesus has to go and complicate things by adding one more idea: flesh. "This bread is my *flesh*, which I will give for the life of the world." (John 6.51) The bread of heaven, Jesus was explaining, wasn't just a relationship with him, it *was* him! And more specifically, it was his body, which he was about to offer up on the cross "for the life of the world". The Jews in the story started getting really nervous when Jesus talked this way, but instead of backing off, Jesus ramped up the discomfort by just going full steam ahead, no holds barred, whole hog, both barrels: "I tell you the truth, unless you eat the flesh of the Son of Man and drink his blood, you have no life in you. Whoever eats my flesh and drinks my blood has eternal life, and I will raise him up at the last day. For my flesh is real food and my blood is real drink." (John 6.53-55)

Jesus, it appears, had never taken a course on how to make friends and influence people! He used two words that pushed the whole situation over the top: *eat* and *real*. He told the people, "You have to eat my flesh or you have no eternal life," and then, just to make sure they didn't confuse it with some spiritual/symbolic idea, he said, "By the way, my flesh is real food." The word translated *real* is *alethes*, and it means "actual," "not mere

66

appearance, but reality" - not symbolism, but the substance itself. Substantial. Hmmmm. Supersubstantial.

Not only did the Jewish antagonists flip out over these words, the Bible says that a whole bunch of Jesus' disciples abandoned him too. It was a hard saying. Too hard for many of them to swallow, so to speak.

Of course, we know the rest of the story. On the night he was betrayed Jesus took bread and blessed it and broke it and gave it to his disciples and said, "This is my body, which is for you; do this in remembrance of me" (1 Corinthians 11.24). The sacrament of Communion was instituted, and the Church has, ever since then, celebrated the real presence of Christ in the breaking of the bread. Lest we think that this Holy Supper is mere symbolism (not "real" or "substantial"), Saint Paul writes, "Is not the cup of thanksgiving for which we give thanks a *participation* in the blood of Christ? And is not the bread that we break a *participation* in the body of Christ?" (1 Corinthians 10.16) Participation: the Greek is *koinonia*: a true sharing in, a fellowship with.

You see, then, when we pray "give us this day our daily bread", we are also praying (in addition to all the other things we've discussed so far), "Feed us with the sacrament of your true presence. Nourish us with the bread that is your body. Give us everlasting life every time we come to your Table."

By now your head may be spinning in circles - this little petition is so full of depth that any given thought about it springs forth into a hundred other thoughts and insights. But by now you may be able to pull these various ideas together and see that what *all* of this points to - our physical sustenance, our spiritual sustenance, our relationship with Jesus, and even the Sacrament of the Body and Blood of Christ - what *all* of this points to - is that final and eternal and unending feast, that never-ending party (think *fiesta*) in the presence of God, toward which those who love him are all moving. That great feast, which has already been tasted in the Holy Eucharist, gets fully under way at the Second Coming of Christ when he restores all things. This is why Saint Paul says, when he speaks of the Sacrament, "For whenever you eat this bread and drink this cup, you proclaim the Lord's death *until he comes*." (1 Corinthians 11.26)

"Give us this day our daily bread". In those few words we are praying for our physical sustenance, for our future provision, for our spiritual food, for our ongoing and daily relationship with Jesus, for him to feed us in the Sacrament, and for us to have the reality of the future Kingdom-Feast foretasted in the here and now. It's all about food. You are what you eat.

Chapter Four
Propitiation
(Adapted from *Salvation And How We Got It Wrong*, Chapter Five)

Propitiation is one of those words no one uses anymore except when talking about religion or theology. I bet you have never used it in normal conversation. It is one of English words that is dying, and most people don't have a clue what it means, only that it has something to do with paying God, making a sacrifice to God, in order to gain his forgiveness. Which is *not* what it means, as we shall discover momentarily.

But, this does bring up the whole question of sacrifices to God in the ancient religions, in Judaism, and in Christianity. Wasn't the religion of ancient Jews filled with sacrifices? Didn't they have to continually offer sacrifices, of animals, of grain, even of alcohol, in order to gain God's favor? Wasn't this all a kind of forerunner to Christ sacrificing himself so God would forgive us? The answer to these questions, in short, is, "NO!"

Propitiation Defined

The word propitiation is used four times in the New Testament, each time referring to Jesus and his self-sacrifice on our behalf.

> Romans 3.25: ...whom God put forward as a *propitiation* by his blood, to be received by faith. This was to show God's righteousness, because in his divine forbearance he had passed over former sins.

Hebrews 2.17: Therefore he had to be made like his brothers in every respect, so that he might become a merciful and faithful high priest in the service of God, to make *propitiation* for the sins of the people.

1 John 2.2: He is the *propitiation* for our sins, and not for ours only but also for the sins of the whole world.

1 John 4.10: In this is love, not that we have loved God but that he loved us and sent his Son to be the *propitiation* for our sins.

The dictionary definition of "propitiation" is,

Propitiation: Noun - The action of propitiating or appeasing a god, spirit, or person.

Propitiate: Verb - To win or regain the favor of (a god, spirit, or person) by doing something that pleases them. Synonyms: placate - appease - conciliate - pacify - mollify.

If we accept at face value the English definition, Jesus died on the cross to "placate, appease, conciliate, pacify, mollify" the Father. That's the definition for the English word, but what does the Greek word behind it really mean? Clearly the writers of the New Testament weren't writing in English. What did *they* mean when they wrote about this subject?

In Greek the word is *hilasterion*. Now, there are two different definitions of *hilasterion*. One definition comes from the pagan world, and one comes from the Jewish world. Ask yourself this question: when Paul, John, and the writer of Hebrews uses the word *hilasterion*, which definition were they using? Were using it like the pagans did, or like the Jews did? (Hint: these writers were all Jewish followers of Jesus.)

In the pagan Greek culture the word is indeed used for appeasing an angry God. Your god is upset with you for something (the ancient gods were notoriously fickle and apt to wake up any morning on the wrong side of the bed), and before your god will send rain for your crops, you have to get him back into a good mood, you have to get on his good side. The way you regain his favor is by sacrificing something to him. It has to cost you. It has to hurt. So, you take your newborn child to the pagan altar, lay her in the hands of your pagan priest, and the priest proceeds to slit her throat and pour her blood out on the altar of the god. Now your god is appeased and will send rain. That is the pagan idea behind *hilasterion*. Sadly, tragically, this is the idea that has crept into much of Christian thinking regarding the word.

But Jews had a different understanding, a different definition. In the *Septuagint* (the Old Testament translation used by the Apostles - the one they quoted when they gave Old Testament references in their writings) *hilasterion* is the word for "mercy seat." Remember, the Ark of the Covenant contained a copy of the Law (*the* copy of the Law), and the mercy seat was the "lid" to the Ark. The Law demands our perfection, but the mercy seat covered those demands - and it was there that blood was sprinkled on the Day of Atonement.

When the New Testament writers use *hilasterion* they are not using it with the pagan definition (appeasing an angry God), rather the Old Testament *Septuagint* definition (covering to protect us in our failure to measure up to the Law). Please go back now and re-read those verses in light of what I've just shared.

So, Christ is the *hilasterion* - the "covering" - that protects us from the curse of the Law. He is the place where the blood of atonement is sprinkled, spilled, shed. Once again, the focus shifts - the idea is not that Christ died to change the Father (isn't he unchanging?), but to change us. His sacrifice of himself, initiated in the very heart of the Father, is our covering and our atonement.

But, what about all those sacrifices in the Old Testament? What about that uncomfortable encounter between God and Abraham when the Lord told him to sacrifice Isaac? That's unthinkable to us. It doesn't jive with our sense of justice or anything else. It seems barbaric. It *is* barbaric. And that's the point. God says, "Offer your son," to Abraham, who is from a pagan culture - that's *the norm* in pagan culture, so Abe says, "Where do you want this killing done?" And God says, "Out on Highway 61." - Oh, wait, a Bob Dylan song popped into my he'd and I digress. Where was I?

Oh yes, so Abraham is going to follow through with the *pagan* tradition, and he gets on top of the mountain and God *stops him*. "Abe, this ain't the way we do things. This is *not* how you relate to me. You don't buy me off by killing your boy. I'm not your father's kind of God." *Paradigm shift* - a God who isn't pleased with the blood of bulls and goats (or children), but who instead sacrifices *himself* for our wholeness.

So, if we approach the word *propitiation* (*hilasterion*) as some kind of religious bribe to appease an angry God, we are making God out to be like the pagan gods who need mollifying. This is not how he describes himself in the least - "longsuffering" and "full of mercy" and "forgiving thousands" and all those other words he uses to describe himself. He is *just* - yes, and *righteous* yes - but a *just* and *righteous* judge *makes things right* - he doesn't need buying off. God isn't the kind of god who demands payment. He specifically teaches us *against* such attitudes (you know - all the "forgive seventy times seven," "love your enemies," and "don't pay back evil with evil" lessons). He is the kind of God who, instead of demanding payment be made, actually sacrifices himself in order to reconcile sinners to himself.

Christ's sacrifice of himself is *not* a sacrifice *to* the Father, but a sacrifice to rescue us from sin. It is not "payment" to an angry deity. It is sacrifice of self in order to save. If you had a child you loved (a son or daughter or niece or nephew) who stepped in front of an oncoming semi-truck, you would sacrifice yourself to save the child, but you wouldn't be offering *payment* to anyone in order to save the child. So it is with the sacrifice of Christ. He is the propitiation - the mercy seat, the covering - *for our sins*, and not the pagan styling of propitiation - paying an angry god.

Jewish Sacrifices

The Jewish religious system revolved around sacrifices, and these were commanded by God for the people of Israel. There are far too many sacrifices for us to get into here, and most of them had nothing to do with sin, and nothing to do with blood. But that is a discussion for another time. Suffice it to say that sacrifices were *central* in Jewish worship.

And yet, we also read in the Old Testament that what God is really after is not sacrifices and burnt offerings, but *relationship*:

> Psalm 40.6-8: In sacrifice and offering you have not delighted, but you have given me an open ear. Burnt offering and sin offering you have not required. Then I said, "Behold, I have come; in the scroll of the book it is written of me: I delight to do your will, O my God; your law is within my heart."

> Isaiah 1.11: "What to me is the multitude of your sacrifices,"says the Lord; "I have had enough of burnt offerings of rams and the fat of well-fed beasts; I do not delight in the blood of bulls, or of lambs, or of goats."

Jeremiah 7.21,22: "For in the day that I brought them out of the land of Egypt, I did not speak to your fathers or command them concerning burnt offerings and sacrifices. But this command I gave them: 'Obey my voice, and I will be your God, and you shall be my people. And walk in all the way that I command you, that it may be well with you.'"

Hosea 6.6: "For I desire steadfast love and not sacrifice, the knowledge of God rather than burnt offerings."

Now, jump to the New Testament. In the Gospel of Mark one of the scribes asks Jesus what is the greatest commandment. Jesus told him, "The most important is, 'Hear, O Israel: The Lord our God, the Lord is one. And you shall love the Lord your God with all your heart and with all your soul and with all your mind and with all your strength.' The second is this: 'You shall love your neighbor as yourself.' There is no other commandment greater than these." (Mark 12.28,29) There is nothing in these two "great commandments" about sacrifices. They are about love and relationship and doing good.

So, the scribe says to Jesus, "You are right, Teacher. You have truly said that he is one, and there is no other besides him. And to love him with all the heart and with all the understanding and with all the strength, and to love one's neighbor as oneself, *is much more than all whole burnt offerings and sacrifices.*" This guy "got it." He understood that what God was looking for was not the technical observation of religious ceremony with sacrifices, but living a life of goodness and loving God. Jesus was impressed with this scribe: "And when Jesus saw that he answered wisely, he said to him, "You are not far from the kingdom of God." (Mark 12.34)

Whatever else we say about sacrifices in the Old Testament, as important as they were, *sacrifices were secondary.* What really

counted was living a loving life toward
God and toward others.

But there is more. The Jews didn't see
sacrifices as actually dealing with sin. The
writer of Hebrews tells us, "For it is
impossible for the blood of bulls and goats
to take away sins" (10.4).

What I have been taught and believed
for much too long is that the Jews see
sacrifices as appeasing God. That fits nicely
with the Penal Substitutionary Atonement
understanding of things. But, it turns out,
what I was taught and believed is wrong.

I decided to go get my information
"straight from the horse's mouth." I wrote
several Jewish scholars with a question.
Here is what I wrote:

> I am a product of Western
> Christianity which has placed a
> strong emphasis on what is called
> *Penal Substitutionary Atonement* - the
> doctrine that Christ died (a) in our

place, (b) as payment of a penalty, (c) to appease God's just wrath.

Now, *early* Christianity doesn't have this doctrine. And later Christians who developed and held to this doctrine use the argument that ancient Jewish blood sacrifices are evidence that God's righteous anger must be appeased. So, can anyone help me? What is the purpose of blood sacrifices in ancient Jewish theology?

I must admit that I was *shocked* by their answers. What they told me, all of them, in a nutshell, is that sacrificing in order to appease God's anger is a concept completely foreign to them, and they see it as a "Christian invention." I pointed out to them that it was a *late* Christian invention, because the early Christians didn't see things this way either.

What purpose, then do the sacrifices serve? One fellow responded, "Strictly speaking it makes no logical sense that God needs anything from us nor that by giving God something we can absolve sins. I understand sacrifices by what they cause *for the people*. As biblical Jews were largely agrarians, sacrifices that involved animals and fruits/vegetables were significant and doing so both inspired awe and demonstrated an amount of relinquishing."

When asked, "Were animal sacrifices made to appease God and avert God's wrath, or were they made to cleanse people from sin?" another Jewish fellow responded, "Neither. Both of your possibilities assume that God is lacking something and requires it of us. The sacrifice is *for the one offering it*. A visceral experience to graft a contact action (with a monetary cost) onto the abstract notion of repentance." Another wrote, "I'll chime in my concurrence with the above answers. To reduce it to a very simplistic level the sin offerings were a punitive measure against the sinner as well as a method to force them to think about what they had done. There is no mystical voodoo going on that the act of the animal sacrifice actually forgives the sin in any way."

Another Jewish friend made it clear for me. He said, "When the Jews in the Old Testament were commanded to offer a lamb, it had to be spotless. This means it couldn't be just any lamb from the flock. It had to be raised separately. It had to be inspected every day and cared for. You had to look it in the eyes. This lamb had a *name* - it was a pet. When you offered it as a sacrifice, it *hurt*. It cost you something. The purposes of sacrifices was not to appease God or buy forgiveness. The purpose of sacrifices was to make you feel the cost and pain of your sin. God is a forgiving God. He doesn't need sacrifices in order to forgive sins, he just needs to be asked. The sacrifices are for us, not for him."

So what? Why do I share all this Jewish thought? What do we *do* with this? Let me conclude this section by bringing the focus back to Christ. If we see his sacrifice as an appeasement, to placate God's wrath, then we are saying something *new* - something neither the Jews nor the early Christians said. If, on the other hand, we see Christ's sacrifice as the same kind of sacrifice a loving parent makes for a child, then the sacrifice isn't *Godward* - it is instead *a selfless act made to accomplish something.* And the "something," in this case, is the doing away with sin. The Son of God took on humanity, took on our infirmity, took on our sin (the spiritual disease) and our sins (the ungodly and wrong thoughts, words and deeds resulting from our condition), took on our very death, and bore them all on the cross. He sacrificed himself for us. Or, as the writer of Hebrews says, "He put away sin by the sacrifice of himself" (9.23).

Finally, we *are* guilty of sin, and his sacrifice of himself causes us to see the great cost of our wickedness. But again, sacrifices *are for us*, not for God. Christ offered himself for our guilt, and the sacrifice of his life brings us to love him more, serve him more, and say no to the things and ways of the world which are opposed to the things and ways of God. Saint Paul put it this way, "For the grace of God has appeared, bringing salvation for all people, training us to renounce ungodliness and worldly passions, and to live self-controlled, upright, and godly lives in the present age, waiting for our blessed hope, the appearing of the glory of our great God and Savior Jesus Christ, who gave himself for us to redeem us from all lawlessness and to purify for himself a people for his own possession who are zealous for good works." (Titus 2.11-14)

Chapter Five
Begotten
**(Adapted from *What Christians Believe*,
Chapter Three)**

The knock on my door came in the middle of the afternoon. Two nicely dressed young men in white shirts and dark ties asked if they could come in and talk to me about Jesus. They were riding bicycles. Theologically speaking, I had both barrels loaded. We met for several weeks, once a week, and I pretended to be a novice with lots of questions. But I had special questions that threw them into disarray. Toward the end of our sessions, one of them was transferred away, and I later learned that this was standard operating procedures when one of their missionaries began to doubt what they were espousing.

The various cults which lay claim to the name "Christian" usually share one thing in common: they reject that Jesus Christ is God come in the flesh. But they are tricky. They will say, "I believe that Jesus is the Son of God." And it all sounds so good. But when you put them on the spot and reply, "Well, that's just wonderful! Let me ask you, do you believe that Jesus Christ is God the Son?", they will almost always backpedal and confess that this is *not* what they believe. Do you notice the subtle difference? To say that Jesus Christ is the Son of God can mean almost anything. On some level Adam was a son of God. Kings are called "sons of God" in the Old Testament. So are angels. But to say that Jesus Christ is God the Son is an entirely different statement. It is saying that Jesus *is*

God, pure and simply. Not that he is *from* God or he is *like* God but that he *is* God.

The heresies of our own day are not new. They have been around for a long time. Arius was a 4th century heretic who said he believed the Apostles' Creed: "I believe in Jesus Christ his only Son our Lord...". But he adamantly refused to say that Jesus was God the Son. Hence the Council of Nicea in A.D. 325, and hence the full definition of who Jesus is that we find in the Nicene Creed:

> I believe...in one Lord Jesus Christ, the only begotten Son of God; begotten of his Father before all ages, God of God, Light of Light, True God of True God; begotten, not made; being of one substance with the Father; by whom all things were made: who for us and for our salvation came down from heaven, And was incarnate by the Holy

Spirit of the Virgin Mary, and was made man.

The first clause of the Creeds addresses the reality of God the Father. There is one God, period. He made everything and upholds everything by his power. The second clause turns our attention to the person of God the Son.

Our Lord

The opening statement about Jesus in the Apostles' Creed seems to say it all, and most Christians would understand it to say that Jesus is God come in the flesh. But Arius and other early heretics claimed to be able to agree with the creedal statement while not embracing the deity of Christ. Here, then, are some ways they could read it:

Just A Man: "Jesus was mortal." He was just a man. Special, yes, but still a mortal.

Maybe not a "mere" mortal, but a mortal.
The cultists of past and present will even
concede that he was miraculously born of a
virgin (with which, oddly enough, Muslims
agree), but he is still made of only the same
stuff we are all made of, humanity. They
see him as unique in that God has specially
chosen him, and he is therefore called the
Son of God, but he isn't God
himself.

just God. Some of the heretics actually
 Jesus is truly
 me a man. He
only appeared to was God
dressing up in human form for thirty three
years, but on the cross the deity departed
from the human body and Jesus died as a
mere mortal.

These false teachings completely missed
out on the deeper meaning of the word
Lord. This next bit is a little technical, but it
is very important. When God revealed his
name to Moses (in Exodus 3.14) he said he

was "I AM"; "I BE"; "I EXIST". It was a huge statement in a few words. God declared that he simply IS. He has no beginning and no end. He depends on nothing else for his being. Everything else is made, he is the Unmade. We call ourselves human *beings*, but we aren't, really. We are human *becomings* - we are always changing, growing, modifying, dying. Unlike us (or anything else in creation) God "BEs". He IS.

So when God gave his name as "I AM" it became a sacred name. The Jews thought it so sacred that they refused to write the whole word and left out the vowels, leaving only the consonants: Y...H...W...H. Nowadays no one even knows what the vowels were, so different Bible translations put different letters in between the consonants: YeHoWaH: "Jehovah" or YaHWeH: "Yahweh". When it came to saying the name of God it was considered unpronounceable, so the Jews substituted the word *Adonai*, that is "Lord". Even today in many English translation you will read about the LORD God. Notice that the word LORD is in all capitals; this is a way to signify in English the sacred name of God.

When the Old Testament was first translated into Greek (in 300 B.C.) the translators translated *Adonia* using the Greek word *kurios,* which means lord or master or governor. Later, when the Apostles wrote the New Testament in Greek, they also used the word *kurios* or *Lord* in reference to Jesus. But they weren't saying that Jesus was simply a master, or a governor. They were saying that Jesus was *Adonia.* That Jesus was Jehovah. That Jesus was Yahweh. That Jesus was *one and the same* with God!

When doubting Thomas, who missed out on seeing the risen Jesus with the rest of the Apostles, finally encountered him, he put his fingers into the wounds of Jesus and declared, "My *Lord* and my *God!*" (John 20.28) When Saint Stephen was being stoned to death, he cried out, "*Lord* Jesus receive my spirit." (Acts 7.59) When the disciples baptized people into the Christian faith they baptized them in "the name of the *Lord* Jesus." (Acts 8.16) The declaration repeatedly made by the Apostles throughout the book of Acts was regarding "the *Lord* Jesus." (9.17, 10.36, 11.20, 15.11, 15.26, 20.21, 28.31) When Paul told people how to be saved he said, "Believe in the *Lord* Jesus and you will be saved..." (Acts 16.31) When Saint Paul wrote about Jesus he said things like:

> "If you confess with your mouth, "Jesus is *Lord*," and believe in your heart that God raised him from the dead, you will be saved." (Romans 10.9)

> "The God of peace will soon crush Satan under your feet. The grace of our *Lord* Jesus be with you." (Romans 16.20)

"To the church of God in Corinth, to those sanctified in Christ Jesus and called to be holy, together with all those everywhere who call on the name of our *Lord* Jesus Christ—their *Lord* and ours." (1 Corinthians 1.2)

"There is but one *Lord*, Jesus Christ, through whom all things came and through whom we live." (1 Corinthians 6.8)

The title "Lord Jesus" is used 101 times in the New Testament. It is a magnificent declaration that Jesus is the One who made all things, and who has now come among us, born of a Virgin. But none of this mattered to the false teachers, and so two hundred years after the Apostles' Creed was formed, the Nicene Creed expanded on the idea, and left no wiggle room for heretics.

Begotten of His Father Before All Ages

Most people see the word "begotten" and automatically think "born". But begotten doesn't mean born. Birthing is something that happens from the female gender. Begetting is something that happens from the male gender. It takes two - the male begets - that is, he gives his seed, and the female births - that is, she brings forth. When the Bible says that Jesus is "the only begotten Son" it is not in any way a reference to what happened with the Virgin Mary or with his birth. It is a statement of his relationship to God. The Hebrew word literally means "brought forth" or "published". God the Son wasn't begotten in Bethlehem! He was begotten, as the Creed says, "eternally". Eternally means forever - past, present and future, outside time. God the Son has *always* been "published" or "brought forth" by the God the Father. The prophet Micah used the same word when he prophesied that the Messiah would be born in Bethlehem, he wrote, "But you, Bethlehem Ephrathah, though you are small among the clans of Judah, out of you will come for me one who will be ruler over Israel, whose *origins* (other translations say *"generations"* or *"goings forth"*) are from of old, from ancient times (or "from days of eternity")." (Micah 5.2) There never was a time when he wasn't begotten. The "begottenness" of God the Son did not begin at creation, nor at his birth as a man. He was begotten "before all ages" - before time - eternally. He was not begotten at a point in time, or even at a point before time (a logical impossibility). He was, is and will be always "being brought forth" from the Father.

He is indeed the *only* manifestation of the Father - the *"only begotten* Son" - so that when God is seen, heard, touched - wherever and whenever God is encountered at all - it is proper to understand this as the Son showing forth the invisible "interior" God - the Father (cf. John 1.1,14,18, 6.46, 14.7-9).

God from God...
One Substance with the Father

The Son is not another "entity" from the Father. There are not two Gods (or three). The Son is not someone or something "other than" the Father. The Creed establishes the Scriptural teaching that the Son is "God from God...true God from true God". The emphasis here is on the union of the Father and Son, and this idea culminates with the overarching phrase, "being of one substance with the Father". The Greek here translated "one substance" is *homoousion*; "same substance." There is only one substance, one "stuff" of God, and it is God himself. Deity isn't spread around throughout the universe. God is omnipresent (in all places - this doesn't mean that God is so *big* that he fills up everywhere, it means that God is fully and totally everywhere at once. All of God is here and all of God is there, he fills all in all). There are not batches of divinity parceled out. There is simply the stuff of God, the substance of God, and it is one because *he* is One.

When the Creed proclaims that the Son is "of one substance with the Father" it means there is no division between them. In these short words we find a reaffirmation of the *Schema* in Deuteronomy 6.4: "Hear O Israel the Lord our God, the Lord is one." God the Son is the manifestation of that One God, whether that happened in the Old Testament (creation, God's appearances to Moses and others, etc.) or the New Testament, when "the Word was God...[and] the Word became flesh" (John 1.1-14).

By Whom All Things Were Made

Just to make sure they weren't misunderstood, the writers of the Nicene Creed went on to say that it was the Son who made everything. We have seen in the first clause of both Creeds that God the Father is the maker of heaven and earth. Now we are told that God the Father (that invisible, unseeable, untouchable, inner reality of God that dwells in light unaccessible - cf. Exodus 33.20, Judges 13.22, Matthew 6.6, 18, John 1.18, 6.46, 1 Timothy 6.16) has created all things *by* and *through* God the Son - God made manifest.

The Incarnation

We now come to the central truth of Christianity: "Who for us and for our salvation came down from heaven". God the Son, the very manifestation of the invisible God himself, the one who is the

Word of God and brought all things into existence, the one who revealed himself to Moses and Joshua and the Prophets, "came down from heaven." And his coming from the heavenly dimension into our realm of the physical was not just for a visit, but for an eternal union with what he had made, and in particular with humanity. But it must be emphasized that this wonderful act was not for himself - he didn't "need" to join himself to us - he did it for "us and for our salvation." The very act of the incarnation ("enfleshing") was to save creation and restore mankind to himself. It was an act of love.

How he came down from heaven was that he became "incarnate by the Holy Spirit of the Virgin Mary". The Spirit of God is referenced as that life, that energy, that "flow" between the Father and the Son, and it was by the Spirit that the Son became flesh. The angel Gabriel appeared to the Virgin Mary and told her, "The Holy Spirit will come upon you, and the power of the Most High will overshadow you. So the holy one to be born will be called the Son of God." (Luke 1.35)

And so, for us, was God "made man." In the womb of the Virgin Mary God joined himself to his creation. He took the flesh of Mary - her egg, and joined himself to her flesh and the child born was without human father but was of human mother. "The Word became flesh." (John 1.14) In the early Church the Virgin was given the title, "Mary, Mother of God." Some people have been thrown off by this title, feeling that it elevated Mary to too high an honor. Laying aside for a moment that the Bible actually says that all generations will call her Blessed and that she is blessed among all women (Luke 1.42, 48), the title is not about Mary, but about Jesus. The title is not a marian statement, but a christological statement. It is saying that what was in the womb of Mary was really and truly God, "true God of true God!" In the inner chamber of humanity, in the womb of the Virgin Mary, God became man. He did not simply put on a human costume. He became man. Never again to *not* be man! God elevated the stuff of our nature to the place of Divinity eternally! Jesus Christ is *fully* God and *fully* man and the two shall nevermore be divided or separated. A man - one of us - sits enthroned in the heavenlies *forever* and is God Almighty!

It was all an act of love, a reuniting, a reconciling: "God was in Christ Jesus, reconciling the world to himself, not counting men's sins against them." (2 Corinthians 5.19)

Chapter Six
Holy

(Adapted from *The Trinity Untangled*,
Chapter Two, and *What Christians
Believe*, Chapter Ten)

What do you think when you hear the
word holy? Even better, when you hear the
word holiness? A lot of modern Christians
automatically think it refers to something
relating to morality or ethics or keeping
rules. It doesn't. Not even a little bit. The
word is used first and foremost in regard to
God himself, and only by extension to
people, places, and things. So, before we

unpack the meaning of the word holy, let's talk for a minute about the nature of God.

God is One

The place to start in understanding the nature of God is the simplicity or singularity of God himself. God is one. Deuteronomy 6.4 is the first verse Jewish children memorized. If Christian kids are taught John 3.16 as the verse that capsulizes the whole New Testament, Jewish boys and girls were taught Deuteronomy 6.4 as the verse that capsulized everything Judaism was about. The verse, called the *Shema*, simply says, "Hear O Israel, the Lord our God: The Lord is one."

One day Jesus was talking to a group of men about things theological, and a scribe saw that he was answering well, so though he would weigh in with his own question, perhaps to trip up Jesus in an argument:

One of the scribes...asked him, "Which commandment is the most important of all?" Jesus answered, "The most important is, 'Hear, O Israel: The Lord our God, the Lord is one. And you shall love the Lord your God with all your heart and with all your soul and with all your mind and with all your strength.' The second is this: 'You shall love your neighbor as yourself.' There is no other commandment greater than these." (Mark 12.28-32)

Whatever else Christianity teaches about God, the foundational truth is this: God is one. There are not millions of gods as some Eastern religions hold, there is not a *pleroma* of gods or a hierarchy of gods as some of the Gnostics held, there are not gods mating and making babies who grow up to be gods as the Greeks and Romans held, and there are not three Gods as some of the heretical "Christian" groups held. There is one God. Period. End of story. And that God is holy.

Holy God

One of the words most frequently associated with God in the Old Testament is *holy*:

> 1 Samuel 2:2 There is none *holy* like the LORD: for there is none besides you; there is no rock like our God.

> Isaiah 6.1-3: In the year that King Uzziah died I saw the Lord sitting upon a throne, high and lifted up; and the train of his robe filled the temple. Above him stood the seraphim. Each had six wings: with two he covered his face, and with two he covered his feet, and with two he flew. And one called to another and said: "*Holy, holy, holy* is the Lord of hosts; the whole earth is full of his glory!"

> Psalm 71.22: I will also praise you with the harp for your faithfulness, O

my God; I will sing praises to you
with the lyre, O *Holy One of Israel.*

When we hear the word holy, we tend to
translate it in our minds as *moral* - "Good
old Joe doesn't go out partying or run with
the wrong bunch. He's a really holy guy."
But that isn't what it means. The Hebrew
word for holy is *qadosh* (the Greek is *hagios*),
and it doesn't speak to morality, but to
separateness. It speaks of "the innermost
description of God's nature,"[11] and perhaps
the best English word to use to translate
qadosh is *unique.*

To say that God is holy is to say that he
is separate from everything else that exists.
He is infinite, all else is finite. He is
uncreated, all else is created. He is
completely other. He is transcendent. You
see, of course, how this connects to the idea

---

[11] "As already in the OT, e.g., in the prophets, the ἅγιος
predicate is referred to the person of God. Indeed, it
contains the innermost description of God's nature (Is.
6:3). Thus the *Trisagion* recurs in the song of praise of
the four beasts in Rev. 4:8." (Kittel, TDNT, v. 1, p. 100).

of him being singular. To be unique
requires oneness.

Theologically used, anything else called
holy is so called because of its relationship
to God, whether that be holy ground, a
holy people, a holy vessel, or a holy place.
A thing becomes holy because it is
separated out for God, and is somehow
related to the unique, transcendent,
singular God himself. But if we are
speaking ontologically (that is, regarding
the nature of a thing itself), only God is
truly holy.

Holy People

Holiness has been given a bad name in
modern times. It has been misdefined as
legalism. Let me make it clear here and
now: holiness has *nothing to do* with
legalism. People have assumed that
holiness means not playing certain games,
not drinking certain drinks, not wearing

certain fashions and hairstyles. Nothing could be further from the truth.

When the Bible and the Church speak of being holy, the idea is being *separate*. It means to be set aside for a special purpose. No one drinks root beer from a sacred chalice. The chalice is set aside for a special use - for celebrating the Lord's Supper. Root beer is drunk from an ordinary glass or even a paper cup. The chalice is holy.

This is not a moral statement in any way. The chalice isn't holy because it observes some legalistic set of rules; it is holy because it is set aside for special use. No bride-to-be would wear her wedding dress to go have breakfast at Denny's. First of all, everyone would look at her and think she was crazy. Second, she would spill gravy on it. But more importantly, the wedding dress is set aside for a special purpose - her wedding. That dress is not like other dresses. It is holy.

When God established his own New Covenant people, those people were called his "Church". The Greek term for church (*ekklesia*) is not a religious word at all, but a political one. It has to do with citizenship. It was used for a group of citizens being called out for a special meeting or task. When the New Testament writers use this word they are saying that God's people are a "called out people". God has called us out of the world (the powers that stand in opposition to him) and has called us to stand *over against* the world. The Church is to be defined by its *differentness* from the world. We are to live by God's standards, not fallen man's. We are to hold to God's values, not the values of our particular culture and age.

Saint Paul wrote to the Ephesians, "Consequently, you are no longer foreigners and aliens, but *fellow citizens* with God's people and members of God's household, built on the foundation of the apostles and prophets, with Christ Jesus himself as the chief cornerstone. In him the whole building is joined together and rises to become a *holy* temple in the Lord." (Ephesians 2.19-21)

What does it mean to be a holy people? It means we belong to a Holy God and so we live by the beat of his drum and not the pounding of the many other drums in our world. God is a holy, unique, God. And because we belong to him, we are a holy, unique, people.

Chapter 7
Glory
(Adapted from *The Trinity Untangled*, Chapter Five)

"Well, glory!" I remember preachers from my childhood getting excited and shouting it out. "Glory be!" I'm still not sure what that means or where it came from, but I remember my granny saying it. She said it when she was pleasantly surprised. If she had been a Catholic I might have thought it was shorthand for, "Glory be to the Father, and to the Son, and to the Holy Spirit," but she was Baptist, so it wasn't that. Some people use it as another word for heaven. "When we all get to glory, what a day of rejoicing that will be..."

In the Old Testament the phrase used to denote God himself making himself seen and known is "the glory of the Lord." For example, in Exodus we read,

> So Moses and Aaron said to all the people of Israel, "At evening you shall know that it was the Lord who brought you out of the land of Egypt, and in the morning you shall see *the glory of the Lord*, because he has heard your grumbling against the Lord. For what are we, that you grumble against us?"...And as soon as Aaron spoke to the whole congregation of the people of Israel, they looked toward the wilderness, and behold, *the glory of the Lord* appeared in the cloud. (Exodus 16.6-10)

Notice that the cloud was not the glory of the Lord. The glory of the Lord appeared *in* the cloud. The cloud was a kind of vehicle that God rode around in. In Exodus 40.34 the vehicle pulls up to the Tabernacle, parks, and God gets out: "Then the cloud covered the tent of meeting, and *the glory of the Lord* filled the tabernacle," just like he used to before the Tabernacle was built and the cloud would park at the entrance of the tent of meeting and the Lord would go in and speak with Moses "face to face." (cf. Ex. 33.9-11)

When we think of the word glory we usually think of brilliant light or some numinous and nebulous glow, but the Hebrew word *kabowde* literally means "that which can be weighed." In other words, something tangible; something with physicality; something that was touchable, seeable, hearable. Later it came to mean wealth. A king of "great glory" was a man who had a lot of stuff that could be weighed - gold and silver and precious jewels. But when we read the phrase "the glory of the Lord" we ought to think of it as the transcendent God, the unknowable / unseeable / untouchable Lord, making himself immanent, making himself known and seen and touched.

Ezekiel actually describes precisely what this glory looked like, and what he saw in his heavenly vision is startling:

> And above the expanse over their heads there was the likeness of a throne, in appearance like sapphire; and seated above the likeness of a throne was *a likeness with a human appearance.* And upward from what had the appearance of his waist I saw as it were gleaming metal, like the appearance of fire enclosed all around. And downward from what had the appearance of his waist I saw as it were the appearance of fire, and there was brightness around him. Like the appearance of the bow that is in the cloud on the day of rain, so was the appearance of the brightness

all around. Such was the appearance of the likeness of *the glory of the Lord*. And when I saw it, I fell on my face, and I heard the voice of one speaking .(Ezekiel 1.26-28)

"With a human appearance" - the glory of the Lord, the physical tangibility of God, was seen by Ezekiel to be in the form of a man! We can't leave the subject without pointing out that the prophet Isaiah, when he describes the coming of the Messiah, Jesus, writes, "And *the glory of the Lord* shall be revealed, and all flesh shall see it together, for the mouth of the Lord has spoken." (Isaiah 42.8) When the writer of Hebrews describes Jesus he says, "He is *the radiance of the glory of God* and *the exact imprint of his nature,* and he upholds the universe by the word of his power." (Hebrews 1.3)

The glory of the Lord is not some aura, some glow, some brilliance. It is the manifest presence of the One True God himself, made tangible to his people, the unseeable making himself seen.

In the Old Testament, there are three phrases that connote God manifesting himself: the Word of God, the Angel of the Lord, and the Glory of the Lord. All of these are titles for the same thing: the self-revelation of the transcendent God. God, the Invisible One, making himself visible; the Unknowable One making himself known; the One who is Completely Other drawing near to his creation. In every case of these phrases being used, they are describing the One, Holy God interacting with his creation and his people.

There is one more phrase that dominates the New Testament, one that encompasses and supersedes all these other titles: *the Son of God*. Or, *God the Son*.

Jesus *is* the Glory of the Lord joined to human flesh. This is why the prophet proclaimed, "And *the glory of the Lord* will be revealed, and all people will see it together. For the mouth of the Lord has spoken." (Isaiah 40.5). This is what led John to write, "The Word became flesh and made his dwelling among us. *We have seen his glory, the glory of the one and only Son*, who came from the Father, full of grace and truth." (John 1.14)

Can the word ever mean brilliance or brightness, or blessing, or goodness? Well, yes, it can. Peter declared, "And when the Chief Shepherd appears, you will receive the *crown of glory* that will never fade away." (1 Peter 5.4)

St. Paul wrote, "I consider that our present sufferings are not worth comparing with the *glory* that will be revealed in us... the creation itself will be liberated from its bondage to decay and brought into the freedom and *glory* of the children of God." (Romans 8.18, 21)

But, just like we are holy because we belong to a holy God, we enjoy "glory" because we belong to the God of glory - the

God who has substance and reveals himself to us and joins himself, in Jesus Christ, to his people and his creation forever.

Well, glory!

Chapter 8
Inn

True story: during a church Christmas play, when Mary and Joseph came to the inn looking for a place to stay, the compassionate little boy playing the inn keeper went "off script" and blurted out, "You can have *my* room!"

And why not? In a culture given to hospitality, why wouldn't the innkeeper (never mentioned in the Bible, by the way) not have said to the highly pregnant young woman, "Oh goodness! We're full up, but you can certainly have my own room!"? Or, for that matter…

1. Why didn't Joseph and Mary just head over to Zechariah and Elizabeth's house which wasn't far away?

2. Why didn't one of the shepherds who visited say, "Well, this won't do. Let's take them to our home?"

3. This was Joseph's hometown - wouldn't some cousin, or childhood friend, bring them in for the night?

No options but a stable?

Of course, the Bible never actually says Jesus was born in a stable. It just says there was no room in the inn, and when he was born he was laid in a manger. But watch this...

Not Your Typical Holiday Inn

The Greek word translated "inn" (in the KJV) is *kataluma*. It means "guest room," and so by extension, it can mean inn or hotel - a place with guest rooms. The only other place it's used in the Bible is in Luke 22.11-13. Jesus sent some of the disciples off to town, to make preparation for Passover. He told them to go to a certain place, "'and say to the owner of the house, "The Teacher asks: Where is the *guest room*, where I may eat the Passover with my disciples?" He will show you a large upper room, all furnished. Make preparations there.' They left and found things just as Jesus had told them. So they prepared the Passover." Mind you, Jesus didn't send his disciples to the local Holiday Inn to reserve their banquet room. He sent them to a house.

Archeologists have excavated houses from the time of Jesus, and they are very much the same as some rural Palestinian (and Mexican) farmhouses today: the

whole house is basically a big open room.
The family cooks in this corner, sleeps in
that corner, sits and visits in that other
corner. There's a little "mud room" (that's
what my Wisconsin farmer friends call it)
or "dirt room" (that's what my West Texas
farmer friends call it) at the entrance. You
walk in, take off your dirty farming boots,
then step into the rest of the house. But it's
all one big room. The cow or donkey was
brought in at night and kept in the mud
room. This served the dual purpose of
protecting the animal and adding warmth
to the house. And there was always...yep,
you guessed it...a feeding trough - *a
manger* - for the animals to eat from while
they waited through the night. In addition
to this big room, there was often a "guest
room," a *kataluma*, normally on the second
floor where visiting friends and family
could stay and have some privacy, and a
kind of rooftop balcony where everyone
could sit in the cool of the evening and
visit.

How Do You Read The Story?

So, here are two options for you to choose from when reading the Christmas story:

Option One: Mary and Joseph are dirt poor, head to Bethlehem to register for the census, try to find a hotel room for the highly pregnant Mary, get turned away by the innkeeper, and have to settle for the barn out back.

Option Two: Mary and Joseph go to Bethlehem, Joseph's family town, and immediately make their way to the home of his brother (or cousin or aunt or childhood friend). Because others are there too, the guest room is occupied (and upstairs anyway, and not an ideal place for a woman about to deliver a baby), but the family says, "Hey y'all! Come on in - you can stay *with us*!"

While there, Mary goes into labor. The menfolk are all shooed out of the room and the women folk tend to the birth. When the beautiful baby is born he is wrapped up in nice clean wrappings and laid into the softest place around - the manger full of straw - in the same cozy room!

The shepherds come and visit and worship. Then the wise men come. Here's the *pièce de résistance*: in Matthew 2.10-11, when the wise men from the east came to Bethlehem in search of the savior, "When they saw the star, they rejoiced exceedingly with great joy. And going into the *house* they saw the child with Mary his mother, and they fell down and worshiped him.

(For more about this, and many other wonderful insights, check out Kenneth Bailey's *Jesus Through Middle Eastern Eyes*.)

Chapter 9
Priests

(Adapted from *How Christians Worship*, Chapter Four)

I'm writing this chapter while sitting on a beautiful covered patio outside my room at a hotel in Merida, Yucatan, Mexico. I have actually written six at this same hotel because it is an excellent place to escape the hustle and bustle of everyday life and ministry, a place to think and be creative. In between chapters I can walk a few blocks to the central plaza and find wonderful outdoor cafes for lunch and dinner.

The city of Merida was founded in 1542 and is home to the oldest cathedral on the western continents. On every corner, it seems, is a gorgeous church or palace or government hall which invites the passersby to stop for a moment and look up and take in all the beauty of the architecture.

I'm not telling you this to make you envious or to brag about where I am. I have a point to make, and here it is: every one of these buildings took teamwork to build, and each one of them required some kind of master plan and someone with authority to execute that plan. I wonder what the Catedral de San Ildefonso would look like if folk had just gotten together and said, "Hey, let's build a church," with no plan, and no one in charge of construction. Goodness! There might not even be a straight line or a connecting hallway in the whole place, let alone any kind of symmetry or style or beauty. It would be chaos, and it would be, mostly, nonfunctional. God is a God of order, and he has created a world of order and he has made humans as a people with order innately built into their psyches.[12]

When it comes to everything else in life, we insist on order and structure: we want our eggs cooked a certain way; we want our music to be harmonious; we want our highway traffic to flow without disruption. We never stop to think that for our eggs and music and highways to "work," someone has to be in charge. Someone has to have the authority to tell others what to do and how to do it. But when it comes to church, a lot of Christians rile up at the thought of there being anyone with any kind of real or true authority. Some people like to imagine the church as a conglomeration of members who each have a vote on how things are done and the majority rules. Others see pastors as

---

[12] If you don't believe me, just research Fibonacci numbers and the Golden Mean.

hirelings who do the bidding of the congregation or the board. Some even go so far as to say, "We have no leadership and no one in authority, we are just led by the Spirit."

Even in congregations which *are* locally ordered and structured, oftentimes church structure has been mistakenly understood in two ways, each of which may be compared to a particular form of sea life. The first is the single-cell amoeba which, though highly structured within itself, is responsible and accountable to no one else. The independent church movement tends to look at each congregation as completely autonomous, choosing its own course of spiritual life and doctrine, without reference to any other structure, a denomination of one.

The second is like a jellyfish: a loosely structured grouping of cells (and even individual organisms) which float along as a bobbing blob. In some denominations the structure of leadership is at best minimal, and certainly is not viewed as essential to the life and direction of the church.

Interestingly, churches with these personalities tend to attract people with these personalities. So an independent-minded church may be filled with independent-minded people who have difficulty working together for the betterment of the Kingdom.

Fortunately, there is a biblical and historic model of structure for the Church. Not only has it endured for two thousand years, it is also of apostolic design.

The Priesthood of All Believers

Before anything is said about hierarchy or leadership, it is important to lay the groundwork that, in order to fulfill the ministry of the Church (witness, work, winning, worship), God has chosen to *ordain every believer* into a priesthood called to accomplish these purposes. Our baptism serves, among other things, as an ordination into the common Christian priesthood.

There are two words in the New Testament which get translated into the English word *priest*. The first is *hieros*, and it literally means "one who cuts," that is, "one who makes sacrifices." Now, here is the important thing about this word as it is used by the Apostles: it *always* refers to the whole people of God and *never* refers to a special group within the Church. In other words, when the transition was made between an Old Testament caste of priests who made sacrifices of animals (Levites and sons of Aaron and *not* all Jews) and the New Testament writings about priests, the company of sacrificers is expanded to include all believers!

Saint Peter wrote, to the whole Church, "You also, like living stones, are being built into a spiritual house to be *a holy priesthood*...you are *a royal priesthood*, a holy nation, a people belonging to God..." (1 Peter 2.5,9) If we are all priests (and the Bible says we are), and if there is now no sacrifice of the blood of bulls and goats to be offered, what is the sacrifice we make? In the same text, Saint Peter tells us, "...to be a holy priesthood, *offering spiritual sacrifices*...a royal priesthood...that you may *declare the praises* of him who has called you out of darkness into his wonderful light."

Christians, acting together as an holy priesthood, offer the spiritual sacrifice of praise and thanksgiving to God. The writer of Hebrews instructs us, "Through Jesus, therefore, let us continually offer to God *a sacrifice of praise* - the fruit of lips that confess his name." (Hebrews 13.15)

So we are clear that what we're talking about here is not just lip service, but life service, Saint Paul reminds us, "in view of God's mercy, to *offer your bodies as a living sacrifice*, holy and pleasing to God - this is your *spiritual act of worship*." (Romans 12.1) As the old "Prayer of General Thanksgiving" says, "we show forth thy praise, not only with our lips, but in our lives, by giving up ourselves to thy service, and by walking before thee in holiness and righteousness all our days..."

Our Christian work, our Christian sacrifice, our priestly duty, therefore, is to praise God. Together. As a company of priests. As a congregation of people. As a troupe of holy actors acting out the story of our salvation. And this act is *chiefly* done in what is called *The Great Thanksgiving*, when we come together to proclaim God's Word and feast at his Table; when we come to confess our faith and *participate* in Christ's once and for all sacrifice of his body and blood for the life of the world.

Ordained Leadership

"Whoopie! We are *all* priests," I can hear it now, "and I don't need anyone to tell me how to serve my God!" But wait just a minute! Even the Reformers, who rediscovered that missing jewel of a doctrine, the priesthood of all believers, which had long laid covered over with the dust of medieval clericalism, were careful to make this distinction: it is the priesthood of *all* believers, not the priesthood of *each* believer. We are not offering so many million or billion one-man plays. We are offering epic theater of our thanksgiving. This is not Hal Holbrook doing *Mark Twain*, a single figure on the stage. This is Cecil B. DeMille and "a cast of thousands" doing *The Ten Commandments* - working *together* to create an astonishing production.

And speaking of Cecil B. DeMille, let me mention a few more names in that vein: Fellini; Spielberg; Lucas; Tarantino; Scorsese; Hitchcock - directors who are household names. You may not like what they've done, but you must admit that they are masters in their field. Someone obviously likes what they have done - a lot of someones, in fact. Every great movie and every great play has a great director. In the Church, although the entire cast of believers is a priesthood, and the entire drama is a sacrifice of praise, God has appointed leadership to direct, and he has appointed some among us for the lead roles. Biblically and historically, leadership falls into three offices.

Bishops The Apostles appointed and ordained men to continue their apostolic role of oversight and called them *episkopos* or bishops. The Greek word literally means overseer (*epi* = over; *skopos* = to see [*a la* tele*scope*, peri*scope*, and micro*scope*, and to *scope* out the terrain]). As early as Acts 20, when Paul set in place spiritual leadership in Ephesus, we read, "Keep watch over yourselves and all the flock of which the Holy Spirit has made you *overseers*" (Acts

20.28). Later Paul would write to the Church in Philippi, "Paul and Timothy, servants of Christ Jesus. To all the saints in Christ at Philippi, together with the *overseers* and deacons" (Philippians 1.1). When Paul gave his young protege Timothy (himself a bishop ordained by Paul) instructions for establishing the Church he admonished him, "If anyone sets his heart on being an *overseer*, he desires a noble task" (1 Timothy 3.1).

That first generation of bishops are names spoken with reverence by those who know their legacy: Timothy, Titus, Clement, Polycarp, Ignatius - men ordained by the Apostles themselves, who gave their lives in martyrdom, who preserved the faith in the midst of great persecution, and who passed on not only that faith, but that structure of leadership, which they had received from the Apostles.

Some might say, "Oh, but you're just using the *word* overseer and giving it a meaning different from what the Apostles meant; they simply meant elders, or a group of local leaders in a local congregation." While this is no place for an extended debate about the subject,[13] I would offer two simple responses. First, the Apostles use *another* word for the office of elders (more about that next), and second, the men ordained by the Apostles speak of the office of *episkopos* in precisely the same way I am using it. Case in point: Ignatius of Antioch. Born around the same time that Jesus was teaching, performing miracles, dying and rising again, and dying a martyr shortly after the turn of the first century (fed to lions in Rome), Ignatius was appointed by Peter himself as the Bishop of Antioch. After his arrest, while on his way

---

[13] For those who *are* interested in an extended discourse, I suggest three books in particular: Kirk, K.E. (*et al*), *The Apostolic Ministry: Essays on the History and Doctrine of Episcopacy*, London, Hodder & Staughton, 1962; Lightfoot, J.B., *St. Paul's Epistle to the Philippians*, Peabody, MA, Hedrickson, 1993 (originally published in 1868), of particular interested is the dissertation *The Christian Ministry*, pp. 181-269; Staley, Vernon, *The Catholic Religion*, Harrisburg, PA, Morehouse, 1983

to Rome under lock and key (not unlike Saint Paul before him), Ignatius penned letters to the bishops, clergy and congregations in each town along the path of his journey. In these letters he wrote with clarity about the sacrament of Holy Communion and about the office of the bishop. To offer just one of many examples, Ignatius wrote to the Church in Ephesus - a church which had only a generation before been founded by Paul, which hosted for many years the beloved Apostle John, which had as its first bishop Timothy, and was now overseen by the saintly Onesimus (whom tradition tells us was the same Onesimus who had once been a runaway slave, but later a servant to Paul, and about whom the epistle to Philemon was written),

> "Therefore it is fitting for you to run your race together with the bishop's purpose - as you do. For your presbytery [*body of elders; priests*] - worthy of fame, worthy of God - is attuned to the bishop like strings to

a lyre. Therefore by your unity and harmonious love Jesus Christ is sung. Each of you must be part of this chorus so that, being harmonious in unity, receiving God's pitch in unison, you may sing with one voice through Jesus Christ to the Father, so that he may both hear you and recognize you, through what you do well, as members of his Son. Therefore it is profitable for you to be in blameless unison, so that you may always participate in God."[14]

Bishops, returning to our metaphor, are the directors of the Church. And they are the directors of the worship of the Church. It is the responsibility of the bishops to guard the faith, doctrine and worship of the Church as these have been received from

---

[14] Ignatius' Epistle to the Ephesians, Chapter 4; Sparks, Jack N., *The Apostolic Fathers*, Minneapolis, Light and Life Publishers, 1978, p. 78f.

the Apostles. Typically, and throughout the history of the Church, although bishops have the particular care of a single local congregation, they also oversee a group of churches, called a diocese, which is usually, but not always, geographically based.

Priests Ah! We finally get to the word this chapter is supposed to be about! The office of priest emerged almost immediately in the life of the early Church. Not unlike the "ruler of the synagogue" in the Jewish religion of Jesus' time, Christian priests are the leaders of the local congregations of the Church. When the persecution against Christians began in Jerusalem (cf. Acts 7) two things happened: Christians were dispersed throughout Judea and Samaria and other countries, and the Apostles also were dispersed and began their missionary efforts in other regions. The need soon emerged for representatives of the Apostles (and the bishops who succeeded them) to lead local congregations throughout the world. The book of James, one of the first books of the New Testament to be written, is a pastoral document - a kind of pastor's manual - from James, the bishop of Jerusalem, to the priests ("brothers") who had scattered from Jerusalem after the first great persecution.[15]

And so, almost immediately after the Day of Pentecost (Acts 2), the structure emerged of (1) Apostles doing the missionary work of establishing the Church, (2) Bishops overseeing several congregations (*a la* James in Jerusalem, who was not, by the way, one of the Twelve Apostles), and (3) priests overseeing local congregations under the direction of their bishop.

The word priest (*presbyteros* in Greek, which became *presbyter* in Latin, then *prestre* in Old French, then *prester* in Middle

---

[15] For a convincing argument that the Epistle of James was in fact the very first book of the New Testament to be written, and for an insightful commentary on the entire epistle, cf. Scaer, David P., *James: The Apostle of Faith*, London, Wipf & Stock Publishers, 2004.

English and finally *priest* in modern English) literally means *elder* or *mature one*, and refers to those men who are chosen to lead God's flock because of their maturity in spiritual matters and in God's Word. In the Apostolic Church the office of elder was an ordained office for life, and not an elected office of a congregational representative as is often found in churches today. One of the Apostles' jobs in establishing the Church was the appointing of priests or elders for the congregations: "Paul and Barnabas appointed [*ordained*] *elders* for them in each church and, with prayer and fasting, committed them to the Lord, in whom they had put their trust." (Acts 14.23) When the Apostle Paul sent Bishop Titus to Crete, he wrote, "The reason I left you in Crete was that you might straighten out what was left unfinished and appoint [*ordain*] *elders* in every town, as I directed you." (Titus 1.5) Later, the aged Apostle Peter would write to the congregations under his care, "To the *elders* among you, I appeal as a fellow *elder*, a witness to Christ's sufferings and one who also will share in the glory to be revealed: Be shepherds of God's flock that is under your care, serving as overseers - not because you must, but because you are willing, as God wants you to be..." (1 Peter 5.1f)

The priest's duties include caring for the local congregation, celebrating the sacraments, and teaching and preaching God's word, under the direction of the bishop. He is, using the analogy of theater, a leading man in the drama of worship.

Deacons The final office of leadership finds its birth in Acts 6, when seven men were chosen to be servants on behalf of the Apostles to the Church. A situation arose in the earliest days of the Church when widows needed caring for, and things were being mishandled because of a lack of organization. Finally the Apostles ordained seven men, chosen from among the congregation in Jerusalem, to "wait tables" and care for the widows in their need. The office was originally designed to free the Apostles from the daily cares of the congregation, so they could spend time in prayer and study. Taking the name of the office from the Greek word for servant (*diakonos*), these men were called deacons.

Later, Paul would include them when he wrote and spoke of the leadership of the Church: "Paul and Timothy, servants of Christ Jesus, To all the saints in Christ Jesus in Philippi, together with the overseers and *deacons*..." (Philippians 1.1) To Bishop Timothy the Apostle wrote, "*Deacons, likewise, are to be men worthy of respect, sincere, not indulging in much wine, and not pursuing dishonest gain*..." (1 Timothy 3.8)

In much of the modern Protestant Church the role of deacon is that of a lay representative elected by the congregation to serve a few years in the church's leadership - usually hiring or firing the pastor. In the biblical and historic model, deacons are the hands, eyes, and ears of the bishop, ministering on his behalf to the church, and honored to serve, not only at the table of the widows, but at the Table of the Lord. The deacon's stole, worn across his shoulder and tied at the waist, is a symbol of the servant's towel. Going back to the analogy of theater, the deacon might be seen as not only an actor in the drama of redemption, but also as an important stage-hand, making sure everything is ready and in order, so the people of God can offer the sacrifice of thanksgiving.

There are other ministries in the Church, there are other roles and offices, but these are the three *ordained* offices. The bishops, priests and deacons serve as a kind of skeleton or framework on which the rest of the Church's ministry is built. Together with this leadership, the entire people of God work in unity to bring about the witness, work and worship of the Church of God.

Chapter 10
Meet

(Adapted from *The End Is Near...Or Maybe Not!*, Chapter Twelve)

This chapter, and the unpacking of the word "meet," focuses on what the Bible tells us about the end of time. Paul writes that, "After that, we who are still alive and are left will be caught up together with them in the clouds to *meet* the Lord in the air And so we will be with the Lord forever." (1 Thessalonians 4.17) I grew up in a religious tradition that was somewhat obsessed with "the Rapture." As a young "preacher's kid" I used to help my dad study for his sermons about the Rapture.

The short version of this doctrine (properly called Dispensationalism) is that, toward the wrapping up of all history, Jesus will return and catch away those who believe in him (along with all the dead in Christ), and we will *meet* the Lord in the clouds, leaving the world to go to hell in a handbasket in something called the Great Tribulation. After that seven years of chaos, Jesus will return riding on a white stallion for the Second Coming, his people following behind riding on heavenly horses. This is when Jesus and his heavenly host battle against the antichrist and his minions. We win, of course, and Jesus sets up his kingdom, ruling on earth for 1,000 years (the Millennium), basing his operation out of a rebuilt temple in Jerusalem. After that is judgment day, and the new creation.

I believed it. I immersed myself in the teaching. Later, as a young pastor, I taught it. A lot. And then it all started unraveling for me. The deeper I studied the less sense it made. When I was about 25 I came to a crisis in my faith - not my faith in God, but my faith in the only teaching about the end that I had ever heard. I started on a quest to discover what the people of God had believed throughout the centuries, and it was far different from my crumbling position

The Second Coming

This scenario has Jesus returning 1,007 years before the new creation (before, that is, the seven year Great Tribulation and the 1,000 year Millennium). But as I studied more, it became clear that the *last thing* in history as we know it is the return of Christ. When Peter preached his second sermon in Act 3, he declared that Jesus, "must remain in heaven until the time comes for God to restore all things..." (Acts 3.21) This verse alone squashes the Rapture/Tribulation/2nd Coming/Literal Millennium idea. He must remain in heaven until the restoration of all things. The last thing on the timeline is the return of Christ.

Paul lays out the scenario clearly:

> "But in fact Christ has been raised from the dead, the firstfruits of those who have fallen asleep. For as by a man came death, by a man has come also the resurrection of the dead. For as in Adam all die, so also in Christ shall all be made alive. But each in his own order: Christ the firstfruits, then at his coming those who belong to Christ. Then comes the end, when he delivers the kingdom to God the Father after destroying every rule and every authority and power. For he must reign until he has put all his

enemies under his feet. The last enemy to be destroyed is death. For 'God has put all things in subjection under his feet.' But when it says, 'all things are put in subjection,' it is plain that he is excepted who put all things in .subjection under him. When all things are subjected to him, then the Son himself will also be subjected to him who put all things in subjection under him, that God may be all in all" (1 Corinthians 15.20-28)

A Meeting In The Air

OK, OK, already! Some of you have been sitting on pins and needles wanting to ask, "But what about 1 Thessalonians and our being 'caught up to meet the Lord in the air?'" Here's your answer. It will happen. At the Second Coming and not a second before.

But what is immensely important is the *reason* for the catching up—the meeting itself is the big deal, and not the trip to heaven that we read into the text. If we think the catching up is to whisk us away, we completely miss the point.

The word translated "meet" is *apantesis*, and it has a very special meaning. It is used on three occasions in the Bible. The first is in the story Jesus told about the Ten Virgins, when the bridegroom is headed in to town and the cry goes out, "Here is the bridegroom! Come out to *meet* him." (Matthew 25.6) Don't think for a moment that they were going out to meet the bridegroom in order to go away with him.

The second place the word is used is when Paul, in chains, along with Luke and some others arrive in Rome. The Christians there hear Paul and his company are arriving and, "came as far as the Forum of Appius and Three Taverns to *meet* us." (Acts. 28.15) Don't think for a minute that these Roman Christians were going out of the city to meet Paul and go away with him.

The final place the word is used is the passage we're looking at in 1 Thessalonians, the one everybody has wanted to know about since this chapter began:

> "But we do not want you to be uninformed, brothers, about those who are asleep, that you may not grieve as others do who have no hope. For since we believe that Jesus died and rose again, even so, through Jesus, God will bring with him those who have fallen asleep. For this we declare to you by a word from the Lord, that we who are alive, who are left until the coming of the Lord, will not precede those who have fallen asleep. For the Lord himself will descend from heaven

with a cry of command, with the voice of an archangel, and with the sound of the trumpet of God. And the dead in Christ will rise first. Then we who are alive, who are left, will be caught up together with them in the clouds to *meet* the Lord in the air, and so we will always be with the Lord." (1 Thessalonians 4.13-17)

Don't think for a minute that we're going out to meet the Lord so we can go away with him.

The word "meet" (*apantesis*) is a special word which means to go out to welcome an incoming dignitary. The virgins go out to welcome the bridegroom to the festivities. The Roman Christians go out to welcome Paul to their city. All of us Christians (living and dead) on the Last Day, go out to welcome King Jesus home. And in that moment, heaven and earth will be made one. And the New Creation will have been completed. "And so we will always be with the Lord," Paul writes.

We Christians aren't living and waiting for a rescue out of this world. We are living and working and actively waiting for Christ to return, for us to share in his Resurrection, for us to put on immortality, and for all things to be made new. What a meeting it will be!

Chapter 11
Angels and Gather
Adapted from *The End Is Near...Or Maybe Not!*, **Chapter Seven)**

I used to be a big Rapture guy. I grew up hearing sermons about how the Rapture (the secret catching away of Christians from the earth) was going to happen soon. It actually brought angst into my teen years. "Lord, please don't let it happen before I date a girl!" "Lord, please don't let it happen before I get married and have sex!" "Lord, please don't let it happen until I experience being a daddy." I was conflicted, because on the one hand I was praying for God to postpone things a while, but on the other hand I was supposed to be praying, "Even so, come, Lord Jesus."

When I was about 25, married and with three children, I abandoned the popular "Left Behind" theology and embraced something older, more sensible, and more biblical. Then I really started studying the subject. A Bible school published a study manual I had written about it. I preached on it. Then I started doing seminars on the matter and eventually wrote a book (from which the following is adapted).

One very important chapter for understanding eschatology (that's the fancy word for "end times") is Matthew 24, or Jesus' "Olivet Discourse," when he sits on the Mount of Olives and starts teaching about a looming catastrophe. He uses language borrowed from the Old Testament prophets and if you read it literally it sounds like the end of the world.

The monkey wrench thrown into the machinery of popular end times thinking is that Jesus makes clear several times that he is speaking about something that is going to happen soon - in the lifetime of the people listening to him. He isn't telling them about an event thousands of years down the road, he's telling them about an event forty years down the road, something their children and grandchildren would experience, and maybe even theirselves.

On occasion someone who really is imbedded in the popular Rapture teaching but is trying their best to be open minded will ask me to sit down and walk them through the text verse by verse. It makes for an interesting lunch appointment. Interestingly enough, as we journey down through the verses they may not agree with what I'm sharing, but they at least see that it makes sense. Then we come to this verse.

"*Don't tell me* you think this *next* verse was fulfilled in the first century!" I always take a deep breath, say, "Yep, I do," and jump into the next thing Jesus says. So, take a deep breath, hold on to your seat, and listen to the words of Jesus:

> "And he will send out his angels with a loud trumpet call, and they will gather his elect from the four winds, from one end of heaven to the other." (Matthew 24.31)

The more you study the Bible, the more you realize that translation is both science and art. Because words are somehow alive, they change, they mean different things depending on their context. Studying the New Testament in Greek is almost like dancing; there is a rhythm, there is movement, there are steps, there is a beauty to it all, and sometimes we can stumble and make a mess of things. In this verse there are two words that mean one thing at first glance, but something different when we look closer: angels, and gather. How we understand them in this context completely determines how we understand what Jesus meant.

Angels

The Greek word for angels (from which we get our English word) is *angelos,* and it means, simply, messenger. When we read it we automatically think it means something like "heavenly being," but it doesn't. Now, the heavenly beings *are* messengers of God, but they are not his only messengers. John the Baptist was a messenger of God. Jesus said of John the Baptist, "This is he of whom it is written, 'Behold, I send my *messenger* before your face, who will prepare your way before you.'" (Matthew 11.10) Care to guess what the word translated messenger is? You got it— *angelos!* One more: "When the days drew near for him to be taken up, he set his face to go to Jerusalem. And he sent *messengers* ahead of him, who went and entered a village of the Samaritans, to make preparations for him." (Luke 9.51-52) Again, the word is the plural form of *angelos*.

The heavenly creatures are called cherubim and seraphim, thrones, powers, dominions and principalities—they are also called messengers, for they do God's bidding and speak for him. But God has other messengers as well. The Apostles and the 70 were the first messengers heralding the Gospel throughout Israel and throughout the world. Why, then, do we automatically read this verse as "He will send out his heavenly creatures..."? Why not read it, "He will send out his messengers"? This passage is a description of what Christ does with the early church. The last thing he says to his disciples is, "Go into all the world"—he sent them out as messengers. In this verse he is describing what will happen— Jerusalem will fall, and with it the Old Covenant will end, but the messengers of God will go out into the whole world—"to the four winds, from one end of heaven to the other"— with the proclamation of the Gospel of King Jesus.

Trumpet Call

Well, shucks. I wasn't intending on writing about this second phrase in this chapter, but since it is sandwiched in between the two words I intended to focus on, if I don't address it someone will get suspicious, so, here we go. "He will send out his messengers," Jesus said, *"with a loud trumpet call."* This describes the action of the Apostles and the early evangelists. These men proclaimed a message that was *not* whispered in a corner. "What I tell you in the dark, say in the light, and what you hear whispered, proclaim on the housetops." (Matthew 10.27) Paul stood before Felix and said, "I am not out of my mind, most excellent Festus, but I am speaking true and rational words. For the king knows about these things, and to him I speak boldly. For I am persuaded that none of these things has escaped his notice, for this has not been done in a corner." (Acts 26.25-27) In Thessalonica, the pagans raged against the Christians, saying, "These men who have turned the world upside down have come here also," (Acts 17.6)

When God calls his own to himself, he does so with trumpets. "In that day from the river Euphrates to the Brook of Egypt the LORD will thresh out the grain, and you will be gleaned one by one, O people of Israel. And in that day *a great trumpet will be blown*, and those who were lost in the land of Assyria and those who were driven out to the land of Egypt will come and worship the LORD on the holy mountain at Jerusalem" (Isaiah 27.12-13). People in Assyria didn't literally hear a trumpet being sounded in Jerusalem. But they were called out by God to gather to Zion and worship him.

Gather

And what will these messengers do, as they proclaim the Gospel as a clarion call? They will "gather his elect" from all over the world. This isn't a Rapture passage, about being caught away, it is an evangelism passage about harvesting souls and nations. The word gather is a combination of two Greek words, both of which you will be familiar, because they have come over into our own language. The first is the prefix *epi*—we use it in epidural, epidermis, epicenter. It means "over." The second is *synagogue*, and it means, well, synagogue. It means "gathering." A Jewish synagogue is a gathering together of Jewish believers for worship. An English equivalent is "congregation."

This word, *episynagogue*, is used by Jesus when he weeps over the city of Jerusalem and cries out, "O Jerusalem, Jerusalem, the city that kills the prophets and stones those who are sent to it! How often would I have *gathered* your children together as a hen *gathers* her brood under her wings, and you were not willing!" And then he finishes with this terrible line: "See, your house is left to you *desolate*." (Matthew 23.37)

Tellingly, the word is used again in the book of Hebrews: "And let us consider how to stir up one another to love and good works, not neglecting to *meet together*, as is the habit of some, but encouraging one another, and all the more as you see the Day drawing near." (Hebrews 10.24-25)

Episynagogue doesn't mean rapture away, it means gather together.

Now, let us revisit the verse in Matthew: Jerusalem is doomed to destruction, the stars are going to fall for the city, the Son of Man is going to come in judgment, because he is enthroned in the heavens as King and Lord, and he is also going to "send out his messengers with a loud trumpet call, and

they will congregate—gather together—
episynagogue—his elect all over the world."

Jesus warned the people of the eminent
demise of Jerusalem. He wept over it, he
sorrowed over the consequences of their
rejecting him and his kingdom. But before
this prophecy of destruction would occur,
before the Temple and the city would fall
into ruins, the Gospel had to go out —as a
witness to the nations; the Apostles and
early Christians had to go all over the
world loudly proclaiming the Good News
—and then the end (of the Old Covenant,
the Temple, Jerusalem) would come.

This Generation

Just in case someone might hear him
and think he was speaking of events a very
long way off, Jesus finishes this section by
saying,

"From the fig tree learn its lesson: as soon as its branch becomes tender and puts out its leaves, you know that summer is near. So also, when you see all these things, you know that he is near, at the very gates. Truly, I say to you, *this generation* will not pass away until all these things take place. Heaven and earth will pass away, but my words will not pass away." (Matthew 24.32-35)

Which generation? *This* generation—the generation Jesus was speaking to. Not a generation 2000 years into the future (*a la* Hal Lindsay, Tim LaHaye, and company), but the people who were standing there listening to Jesus teach.

Everything Jesus described in this text about the Great Tribulation happened within 40 years of him speaking. Christians shouldn't be anticipating horrible days, growing wickedness, the rise of evil powers and an emergency rescue by a secret

Rapture to get us out of here just in the nick of time. We should be looking for the accomplishment of the Great Commission, the triumph of the Church, and the Second Coming of Christ as a victory celebration.

Chapter 12
Coming

"The coming of the Lord." It is a phrase that is used throughout the Bible and has become common in Christian speech. The Greek word is *parousia*, and as you may have guessed by now, it doesn't mean what we commonly think it means. But before we look at the meaning of *parousia*, let's slow down just a hair and take a look at every time it is used in reference to Christ. Whatever you do, please don't lightly skip over all these verses! And, just for the fun of it, as you read these verses, remember that the term "Second Coming" (good and accurate as it is) is not found in the Bible one single time.

Matthew 24:3 And as he sat upon the mount of Olives, the disciples came to him privately, saying, Tell us, when shall these things be? And what shall be the sign of your *coming*, and of the end of the age?

24:27 For as the lightning comes out of the east, and shines even to the west; so shall also the *coming* of the Son of man be.

24:37 But as the days of Noah were, so shall also the *coming* of the Son of man be.

24:39 And did not know until the flood came, and took them all away; so also shall the *coming* of the Son of man be.

1 Corinthians 15:23 But every man in his own order: Christ the first-fruits;

afterwards those who are Christ's at his *coming*.

1 Thessalonians 2:19 For what is our hope, or joy, or crown of rejoicing? Are not even you in the presence of our Lord Jesus Christ at his *coming*?

3:13 To the end he may establish your hearts unblameable in holiness before God, even our Father, at the *coming* of our Lord Jesus Christ with all his saints.

4:15 For this we say to you by the word of the Lord, that we who are alive and remain to the *coming* of the Lord shall not go before those who are asleep.

5:23 And may the God of peace himself sanctify you wholly; and may your whole spirit and soul and body be preserved blameless to the *coming* of our Lord Jesus Christ.

2 Thessalonians 2:8 And then shall that Wicked be revealed, whom the Lord shall consume with the spirit of his mouth, and shall destroy with the brightness of his *coming.*

James 5:7 Be patient therefore, brothers, until the *coming* of the Lord.

5:8 You also be patient; establish your hearts: for the *coming* of the Lord draws near.

2 Peter 1:16 For we have not followed cunningly devised fables, when we made known to you the power and *coming* of our Lord Jesus Christ, but were eyewitnesses of his majesty.

3:4 And saying, Where is the promise of his *coming*? For since the fathers fell asleep, all things continue as they were from the beginning of the creation.

3:12 Looking for and hasting to

the *coming* of the day of God, in
which the heavens being on fire shall
be dissolved, and the elements shall
melt with fervent heat?

1 John 2:28 And now, little children,
abide in him; that, when he shall
appear, we may have confidence, and
not be ashamed before him at
his *coming*.

When we see the word coming, we think
of the process of getting from one place to
another. "Cathy is coming over today."
Well, where is Cathy? Is she driving over,
walking, taking a cab? How long will it
take her to get here? The idea behind the
English word coming includes the idea of
movement, of journeying. There is a Greek
word that means precisely this, and it isn't
parousia. That word is *erchomai* and Jesus
uses it when he tells us to pray, "Thy
kingdom *come*." However, our word for the
day, *parousia*, carries with it nothing of the
idea of transit.

Parousia is made of two words meshed together. The first is *para* and it means "alongside." Jesus calls the Holy Spirit our *paraclete*. That gets translated as "comforter," but it is really a term for a defense attorney. Someone who "stands alongside" us to defend and guide us. We use *para* in English quite a bit, too: *para*llel, *para*chute, *para*graph, *para*trooper. *Para* means beside.

The second word meshed into *parousia* is *ousia*. We've already mentioned it once in this book, in Chapter Five where we discussed Jesus being "of the same substance" as the Father - *homoousion*. *Ousia* means substance, the substantial reality of a thing, the "stuff" that makes the thing the thing.

Put the two words together into *parousia* and what we get is something like, "being substantially present alongside."

We've already looked at every verse where the word is used regarding Jesus, but let's look at verses where it is used in other ways.

1 Corinthians 16.17: "I was glad when Stephanas, Fortunatus and Achaicus *arrived*, because they have supplied what was lacking from you." Paul was wasn't glad that his friends were in the process of journeying to him, he was glad that they were there; they had arrived.

2 Corinthians 7.6, 7: "But God, who comforts the downcast, comforted us by the *coming* of Titus, and not only by his *coming* but also by the comfort you had given him." Paul wasn't comforted by Titus being on a journey, but by Titus' being present alongside him.

2 Corinthians 10.10: "For they say, 'His letters are weighty and strong, but his **bodily presence** is weak, and his speech of no account...'" Paul was here speaking about what his opposition had to say about him. Here *parousia* is translated *bodily presence*. Paul's naysayers weren't saying

his traveling was weak, but his actually being there seemed to show him weak.

Philippians 2.12: "Therefore, my beloved, as you have always obeyed, so now, not only as in my *presence* but much more in my absence, work out your own salvation with fear and trembling…" You get the idea.

A Word Already Pregnant With Meaning

The New Testament is not the first time the word *parousia* is used. It already had weight to it before Jesus and the Apostles used it. It was already a standard word used for the visit of an emperor:

> The *parousia* of the king must have been well known to the people, for there were special payments and taxes to defray the cost of the festivities on that occasion. All over

the world, advent-coins were struck after a *parousia* of the emperor. Advent-sacrifices were offered at these *parousiai*.[16]

What was being focused on here was not the journey the emperor was making to the city, rather his "arrival," his "being there." Clearly, there were preparations to make. The town had to be cleaned up, a fresh coat of paint put on the buildings, roadways repaired. The prophet Isaiah alluded to this idea when he prophesied the arrival of the Messiah: "A voice cries: 'In the wilderness prepare the way of the Lord; make straight in the desert a highway for our God.'
Every valley shall be lifted up,
and every mountain and hill be made low;
the uneven ground shall become level, and
the rough places a plain." (Isaiah 40.3,4)

---

[16] Wuest, K. S. (1997). Wuest's Word Studies From The Greek New Testament For The English Reader (Vol. 18, p. 33). Grand Rapids: Eerdmans

But, wait, there is more! *Parousia* not only already had weight in the Greek world, it also had weight in the Hebrew world. When the Jewish historian Josephus (a contemporary of the Apostles and an eyewitness to the destruction of Jerusalem) described the *shekina* of the Lord (the epiphany or manifestation of the Lord) revealed on Mount Sinai, and later the presence of the Lord being manifest in the Temple, he uses the Greek word *parousia*.[17]

When we read all these New Testament texts about "the coming of the Lord," the focus isn't at all on Christ being "way beyond the blue," and making a trip back to earth! We ought to read these verses, instead, as being about Christ being present, being alongside us, being with us.

---

[17] Josephus, Flavius, *Antiquities of the Jews*, 3.5.2 §80; 3.8.5 §203.

The Real Presence

As sacramental Christians, when we speak of what goes on in Holy Communion, we refer to "the real presence" of Christ being in the bread and the wine. We don't (we *can't*) explain how it happens, but we affirm that it does happen. Jesus is really with us in the Eucharist. The bread and wine really become his body and blood. This is "the Eucharistic *parousia*." Christ is present in the sacrament.

In the liturgy we make the acclamation, "Christ has died, Christ is risen, Christ will come again." Yes, he will come again on the Last Day, but he comes again, he is with us, he is present, every time we gather and celebrate the Eucharist! When we eat and drink the bread and wine, the body and blood, we are participating in a kind of down payment, a foretaste, of that final day when Jesus arrives and makes all things new. We eat the bread of heaven. We participate in the eternal feast, the Supper of the Lamb.

"Oh Lord, come!" The Lord *has* come. The Lord *is* come. The Lord *will* come.

Maranatha

There is a word that St. Paul uses one time in his writings. It isn't a Hebrew word, or a Greek word, but an Aramaic word: *maranatha*. In the closing words of 1 Corinthians, Paul writes, "If any man love not the Lord Jesus Christ, let him be Anathema Maranatha. The grace of our Lord Jesus Christ be with you." (1 Corinthians 16.21,22; KJV)

The King James Version doesn't translate the word, it just leaves it in the Aramaic. Other versions translate it "the Lord has come," "the Lord is come," and, "the Lord will come." Timing is a bit ambiguous in the word *maranatha*.

As you may know, Greek doesn't have punctuation. There are no periods, commas, question marks, or exclamation points. Where to place punctuation is part of the art of translating. The KJV uses punctuation in one way, and I am going to suggest (along with scholars of the Greek New Testament) an alternative, and I believe better, punctuation. Again, the KJV: "If any man love not the Lord Jesus Christ, let him be Anathema [cursed] Maranatha [PERIOD. FULL STOP] The grace of our Lord Jesus Christ be with you." But consider reading it like this instead: "If any man love not the Lord Jesus Christ, let him be Anathema [PERIOD. FULL STOP] Maranatha, the grace of our Lord Jesus Christ be with you."

As I pointed out, Maranatha is a mess when it comes to tense. It can (and does) mean all of these: come Lord, the Lord has come, the Lord is come, the Lord will come. As awkward as it is, since we are speaking of the God, "who was, who is, and who is to come," how about we translate it that way, with all the tenses thrown in? "Come Lord! The Lord has come. The Lord is come. The Lord will come. The grace of our Lord Jesus Christ *be with* you."

Putting It All Together

That is the only time the word is used in Scripture, but it was frequently used in the life of the early church. The oldest known text in Christianity, outside the New Testament writings, is called the *Didache*, or "The Two Ways," or, The Teaching Of The Twelve." It was written sometime near the end of the first century and is a kind of early manual for the conduct of Christian life and worship. Interestingly, it also contains the oldest known description of Christian worship, and in particular of the liturgy of Holy Communion. And - it uses the word *maranatha*! Chapter 10 of the *Didache* includes the prayer that early

Christians prayed after receiving the
Eucharist:

> But after you are filled, thus give
> thanks: We thank You, holy Father,
> for Your holy name which You
> caused to tabernacle in our hearts,
> and for the knowledge and faith and
> immortality, which You
> made known to us through Jesus
> Your Servant; to You be
> the glory forever. You, Master
> almighty, created all things for Your
> name's sake; You gave food and
> drink to men for enjoyment, that
> they might give thanks to You; but to
> us You freely gave spiritual food and
> drink and life eternal through Your
> Servant. Before all things we thank
> You that You are mighty; to You be
> the glory forever. Remember, Lord,
> Your Church, to deliver it from
> all evil and to make it perfect in
> Your love, and gather it from the four
> winds, sanctified for Your kingdom
> which You have prepared for it; for

Yours is the power and the glory forever. Let grace come, and let this world pass away. Hosanna to the God (Son) of David! If any one is holy, let him come; if any one is not so, let him repent. *Maranatha* [Come Lord. The Lord has come. The Lord is come. The Lord will come]. Amen.

The Lord is come! The Lord is here! The *parousia* isn't only about the final "being present" of the Lord, it is something we as the New Covenant people are already engaged in, already participating in, already being blessed by. What happens on that Last Day, the "Second" Coming, is not Jesus getting on a heavenly horse and riding 14 billion light years through the universe to get back to earth. The final coming is about when Jesus, who is one of us, who is born of Mary, and who is also God of God, lays hold of those two realms, the heavenly and the earthly, and brings them together, "till earth and heaven be one," into a new creation, and being with us forever. It is the culmination of what began when Mary became pregnant by the Holy Spirit and gave birth to a son, whom the prophet Isaiah said would be called Immanuel, "God with us."

Chapter 13
Catholic
(Adapted from *What Christians Believe*, Chapter Ten)

I promised with the subtitle of this book that I'd give you a dozen biblical words that probably don't mean what you think they mean. I've done that, with a few extra words thrown in for good measure along the way. But I thought I would make it a baker's dozen and add a 13th chapter. A little lagniappe, as my Louisiana kinfolk say. Except, this time the word we are going to look at isn't a biblical word, it is an early Christian word: catholic.

There are something like twenty five thousand different denominations in the world today. Some of the older ones (and, oddly, newer ones too) claim that they are the only *real* church and that everyone else is at best playing games and at worst going straight to hell.

The first terrible tearing of the fabric of Christian unity came in what is called The Great Schism in the year 1054 when the Church in the West (Rome and the rest of Europe) and the Church in the East (everywhere else - Greece, Northern Africa, the Middle East), had an ugly parting of ways. Since then, particularly in the West, the fragmentation has continued until we end up with what we have today - any given small town has within it at least a dozen different Christian denominations, including the congregations that insist they aren't part of a denomination at all. But before 1054 things were different. Up until that time there weren't different denominations, there was just "the

Church". Some naive lovers of early church history like to imagine the first one thousand years as a kind of heaven on earth, Nirvana, Utopia, when everyone was loving and nice and united and godly. Of course this wasn't the case. Current church fights pale in comparison to the battles and intrigues of the first thousand years. And I even made a gross oversimplification to say that back then there was just "the Church," because even before 1054 there were a couple of unfortunate misunderstandings that ripped the fabric of unity in the Church. But, in spite of all the rivalries, foolishness, deceit, ungodliness, and downright meanness, the one stellar thing that can be said about the early Church that cannot be said fully about the Church today is that it was one.

The older Apostles' Creed declares the Church to be holy and catholic. The later Nicene Creed adds two more markers - she is also one and apostolic. Those have become known, in theological circles, as the four marks of the Church: one, holy, catholic, and apostolic. I'm not going to explore all those words in this chapter, but I am going to hone in on the much misunderstood term, catholic.

Some of you hiccuped when you saw this word. Some of you jumped ahead to this chapter to see what I would say about it. I would propose that many Christians have misunderstood the word. The word, like all words, picks up baggage along the way that sometimes redefines it. As a young man growing up in a quite sectarian Christian tradition, I was assured that some Baptists would make it to heaven, maybe even a few Methodists, but Catholics? Well, clearly not; after all, Catholics worshiped idols, had a form of godliness but denied the power thereof, couldn't go directly to God but had to get to him through a priest, were barnacled over with dead tradition, thought Mary was the fourth person of the Trinity and a goddess in her own right, lived like the devil all week and thought confession on the weekend made it ok, and, maybe worst of all, smoked and drank alcohol. These unfortunate idolatrous souls were going to be busting the gates of hell wide open (and not in a good way). If you happen to be a Catholic Christian, don't laugh too loudly at this description, because there were equally absurd descriptions floating around about us holy roller, tongue talking, snake handling, Bible thumping, Pentecostals. Baptists and Methodists? Meh, they were just kind of half-hearted milquetoast believers, most of whom weren't too serious about being followers of Jesus. But I digress. We were talking about the word catholic. The actual definition of catholic has nothing to do with rosaries, Rome, or Ratzinger (I couldn't resist the alliteration).

DNA

Catholic, defined perhaps a bit oversimplistically, means *universal*. Not just universal in territory - "everywhere" - but universal in time as well. It means that the Church is for everyone in every place in every time.

Now for a less simple explanation. The word catholic comes from the Greek phrase *kath' holou* which means "of the whole" (we get our word wholistic from *holou*). Everyone reading this book has heard of DNA and understands it at least a little bit. DNA is the "code" of our whole body which can be found in any particular part of our body. Scientists can take a cell from my nose or finger or knee - from my blood or skin or bone - and it will contain the DNA code for my whole body - it will tell what color my skin, hair and eyes are; it will tell my weight tendencies, whether I am male or female, what diseases I may be prone to. Amazing stuff, DNA. We might say that, for the human body, DNA strands are *catholic*. They are "of the whole". Each particular DNA strand includes the whole information of the body, just as the whole body is made up of all the tiny particulars. Heady stuff!

In the same way, the word catholic implies that the fullness of the Church can be found in any "cell" of the Church. The first person to apply the word to the Church was not some medieval Roman potentate, but a humble and godly martyr from the first century by the name of Ignatius. He was the bishop of Antioch who was trained and ordained by the Apostles themselves, who found himself under arrest for being a Christian. On his way to being fed to the lions in the Coliseum in Rome, he wrote a letter to the church in Smyrna and said, "Wherever the bishop appears, the whole congregation is to be present, just as wherever Jesus Christ is, there is the *catholic* church" (Smyrneans 8.2). And that's the first time the term was used in regard to the Church.

When we say the Church is Catholic there are several implications. First, it means the Church is *inclusive*. It cannot be catholic and reject people because of race, sex or nationality. When a church refuses someone on the basis of skin color, social status or cultural difference, it loses its catholicity.

Second, it means the church is *dependent*. The Church's expression in a local congregation is not independent. An independent church should be an oxymoron. It should be a contradiction of terms. If the Church is catholic it is not locally independent, but is simply a local expression of the worldwide Church. There is, therefore, a responsibility to interact with and heed the rest of the Church.

Finally, it means the Church is *nonsectarian*. The Church is not distinguished by a unique doctrine, philosophy or practice. The fact that we all have labels is a sad commentary on the state of the Church today. Ideally we should not be identified by whether we are

Charismatic or Pentecostal or Baptist or
Anglican or Roman or Orthodox or any of
the other distinctives that identify us. And
even if we are identified as such, that
certainly should not be the spirit in which
we present ourselves. There should never
be an us/them attitude in the Church. We
are one, we are called out, and we are "of
the whole".

The Quadrilatral

In the Anglican tradition there is
something called the Chicago/Lambeth
Quadrilateral which is a short document
adopted in 1888 that set out four marks for
what it means to be Catholic. The
document isn't infallible, but it's pretty
good. It isn't perfect, but it's a good place to
start.

1. The Holy Scriptures of the Old and
    New Testaments, as "containing all
    things necessary to salvation," and as

being the rule and ultimate standard of faith.

2. The Apostles' Creed, as the Baptismal Symbol; and the Nicene Creed, as the sufficient statement of the Christian faith.

3. The two Sacraments ordained by Christ Himself--Baptism and the Supper of the Lord--ministered with unfailing use of Christ's words of Institution, and of the elements ordained by Him.

4. The Historic Episcopate, locally adapted in the methods of its administration to the varying needs of the nations and peoples called of God into the Unity of His Church.

I would expand point three to include not just two sacraments, but seven, but that's a discussion for another time. If this is a decent description of the DNA or the catholicity of the Church, some of my readers might conclude, "Well, I guess my church isn't Catholic!" I would argue that there are actually degrees of catholicity, but that any church that is truly Christian has at least some of this DNA within it (a commitment to the authority of Scripture, for example), and my prayer is that eventually all of God's church will reclaim its ancient heritage, come into fuller unity, enjoy the riches of a full catholicity, and, as St. Paul wrote, "attain to the unity of the the faith and of the knowledge of the Son of God, to mature manhood, to the measure of the stature of the fullness of Christ." (Ephesians 4.13)

It's a long, long way, but we're gonna get there.

About the Author

Kenneth Myers was born in 1959 in Denison, Texas. The son of a pastor/missionary, he was married Shirley McSorley in 1977 until her death in 2017. They have three children and five grandchildren. He is an Anglican bishop and director of Graceworks Teaching Ministry.

www.kennethmyers.net

Made in the USA
Monee, IL
17 January 2022

89196225R00115